Harness AI's Creative Power to Drive Innovation

Beyond & above ChatGPT: Learn & Leverage AI to bring paradigm shift to transform the businesses

Aishwarya Gupta
Joseph Bulger
Gaurav Aroraa

ARCCHIE

Harness AI's Creative Power to Drive Innovation

AISHWARYA GUPTA
DELHI, INDIA

JOSEPH BULGER
GEORGIA, USA

GAURAV ARORAA
DELHI, INDIA

Editor: Shambhu
Production Manager: Alexa E
Cover design by Freepik
Formatting & Indexing: Gaurav

First Edition: Apr-2024

Reference: 2401018

Published by Arcchie Publications

ISBN-13 (paperback):978-81-966127-4-0

ISBN-13 (ebook): 978-81-966028-7-1

www.arcchieonline.com

TABLE OF CONTENTS

JOIN US ON THE

ARCCHIE PUBLICATIONS

DISCORD SERVER

Connect with fellow readers, authors, and enthusiasts to discuss all things related to our publications and the exciting world of AI, programming, and learning. Share your insights, ask questions, and engage in vibrant discussions to expand your knowledge and inspire creativity. Take advantage of this opportunity to be part of a dynamic community dedicated to exploring the frontiers of technology and innovation. Join our Discord Server today and be part of the ARCCHIE PUBLICATIONS community!

https://discord.gg/z26SenmpEt

DISCOVER YOUR WRITING POTENTIAL WITH ARCCHIE

We all possess unique talents for articulating various subjects, and you're among those gifted individuals. Whether you're a budding writer or a seasoned author, ARCCHIE PUBLICATIONS offers an ideal platform for your creative endeavors. If you aspire to become an author with ARCCHIE, we invite you to explore authors.arcchieonline.com and submit your application today. Our team is dedicated to assisting you in embarking on your authorship journey. Alternatively, scan QR code and connect with us.

FOREWORD

Being an AI driven Hedge Fund owner, AI Marketing Advertisement Coach and ERP Thought Leader (PeopleSoft-Human Capital Management), for more than 21 years, I have had the opportunity to train the Business and Tech leaders on strategic initiatives to create and maximize business partnerships using AI. And, managed the development activities on various multi-million dollar projects.

AI integration in enterprise software like PeopleSoft HCM (Human Capital Management) can offer several advantages and improvements to the overall functionality and user experience. Here are some ways AI can be used in PeopleSoft HCM and AI driven Hedge Fund:

1. Recruitment and Talent Acquisition: AI can streamline the recruitment process by automating candidate sourcing, screening, and matching.

2. Employee Onboarding and Training: AI can facilitate the onboarding process by providing personalized training modules and resources based on the new employee's role and skill set.

3. Performance Management and Employee Engagement: AI can assist in tracking and analyzing employee performance data and team productivity.

4. Predictive Analytics for HR: AI can analyze historical HR data to predict future workforce trends, such as employee turnover, performance, and retention rates.

5. Workforce Planning and Succession Management: AI can assist in workforce planning by analyzing employee skills, performance, and career aspirations.

6. Stock Earnings Predictions using AI for Hedge Fund: Identify the stock options based on the overall industry trends, market indexes, futures, fundamental and technical analysis, for earnings trades.

    - Fundamental analysis attempts to identify stocks offering strong growth potential at a good price by examining the underlying company's business. This analysis relies on information that spans years.

- Technical analysis uses data from short periods of time to develop the patterns used to predict securities or market movement.

In this era of unprecedented technological advancement, the role of artificial intelligence (AI) has emerged as a beacon of innovation, promising to revolutionize the way we live, work, and interact with the world around us. From the seamless integration of AI-powered virtual assistants into our daily routines to the groundbreaking applications of machine learning in Stock Trading world and Enterprise Software, the potential of AI knows no bounds. As we stand on the threshold of a new digital frontier, this book serves as a guiding compass, navigating the complex landscape of AI advancements while also raising critical questions about the ethical considerations and societal implications that accompany this remarkable journey. With a focus on envisioning an inclusive and sustainable future, this book aims to inspire a collective dialogue on harnessing the transformative power of AI for the betterment of humankind.

This book provides a comprehensive and accessible exploration of AI, offering insights into its multifaceted impact and encouraging readers to contemplate its potential for shaping a more inclusive and sustainable future. It focuses on the progress, challenges, and future potential of artificial intelligence (AI) in various aspects of our lives.

It is a great read as it covers various aspects of AI:

1. Introduction to AI: Begin with an overview of what AI is, its historical development, and its transformative impact on diverse fields, including technology, healthcare, finance, and more.

2. Current State of AI: Discuss the current state of AI research, highlighting recent breakthroughs, key technologies, and notable applications that are shaping the present landscape of AI.

3. AI in Everyday Life: Explore how AI is already integrated into our daily lives, from virtual assistants and personalized recommendations to smart home devices and autonomous vehicles, emphasizing its role in enhancing convenience and efficiency.

4. Challenges and Ethical Considerations: Delve into the ethical and societal challenges posed by AI, including issues such as algorithmic bias, data privacy, job displacement, and the potential misuse of AI technology, while also addressing the importance of responsible AI development and regulation.

5. AI and the Future of Work: Discuss how AI is reshaping the workforce and job market, examining the potential opportunities and challenges for individuals, businesses, and industries, and proposing strategies for upskilling and adapting to the evolving job landscape.

6. AI and Sustainability: Examine how AI can contribute to sustainable development and environmental conservation, discussing its applications in areas such as energy efficiency, climate modeling, and natural resource management, and highlighting its potential to address pressing global challenges.

7. Emerging AI Trends: Highlight emerging trends in AI research and development, including advancements in quantum computing, explainable AI, and AI-driven automation, and speculate on their potential impact on various sectors in the near future.

8. AI and Society: Discuss the broader societal implications of AI, including its influence on governance, education, and cultural dynamics, while also considering the importance of fostering public understanding and awareness of AI technologies.

9. A Vision for the Future: Conclude by envisioning a future where AI is harnessed for the collective good, emphasizing the need for collaborative efforts between policymakers, technologists, and society at large to ensure that AI development is guided by principles of inclusivity, fairness, and sustainability.

Warm Regards,
Ajay Bhowmick- Founder & CEO, AI Enthusiast
https://linkedin.com/in/ajbhowmick

DEDICATED TO

To my family, friends and colleagues who embodies the essence of friendship, mentorship, and collegiality. I dedicate this book to the pioneers whose visionary strides propelled artificial intelligence into reality. To the unsung researchers tirelessly pushing the boundaries, and to the educators demystifying this complex field, this dedication honors your relentless pursuit of knowledge. To the innovators who see AI not just as a technological marvel but a force for societal good, your ethical compass guides our advancements. To the future generations, may this dedication inspire you to harness AI's power responsibly and ethically, shaping a world where intelligence augments humanity. This book is dedicated to those whose passion and dedication forge a brighter AI-driven tomorrow.

- Aishwarya Gupta

With profound gratitude, I dedicate this book to my lovely family, whose unwavering support and boundless love have been the foundation of my journey as a writer. You have been my constant source of inspiration, and this book is a tribute to the warmth and strength you have infused into my life. Thank you for being my pillars of strength, my biggest cheerleaders, and the embodiment of the love that fuels my creativity. This book is as much yours as it is mine.

- Joseph Bulger

To all my friends and colleagues, I want to express my gratitude for your steadfast support, encouragement, and inspiration, which have served as the driving force behind the creation of this book. Whether it was your direct assistance, valuable insights, or the simple gift of your friendship, you have played an essential role in bringing these words to fruition. This book stands as a testament to the shared journey we've embarked upon, and I am deeply thankful for your contributions, both apparent and concealed.

- Gaurav Aroraa

ACKNOWLEDGMENTS

Writing a book is a journey that spans beyond the solitary act of putting words on paper. It's a collaborative effort, a tapestry woven with threads of inspiration, guidance, and unwavering support.

First and foremost, I express my heartfelt gratitude to my daughters Prashita & Shreeya who supported and stood by me on this journey to give me strength for completing this book on time, my friend Ajay, whose unwavering belief in the power of knowledge and innovation has been my guiding star throughout this endeavor. Your boundless encouragement and invaluable insights have been a constant source of inspiration.

I extend my sincere appreciation to many of friends, whose mentorship has been instrumental in shaping my understanding of the complex world of Generative AI. Their willingness to share expertise and provide clarity amidst intricate concepts has been truly transformative.

My gratitude also extends to the team at Archie Publication, for their dedication, enthusiasm, and unwavering commitment to bringing this book to fruition. Your expertise and tireless efforts have transformed my vision into a tangible reality.

To my colleagues and peers who offered their insights and feedback, thank you for your thoughtful contributions that enriched the content and depth of this book. Your collective wisdom has left an indelible mark.

I am deeply appreciative of the individuals who participated in interviews, shared their experiences, and allowed me to weave their stories into the narrative. Your real-world perspectives have lent authenticity and depth to these pages.

Finally, my gratitude goes out to the readers – both novice and expert – who will embark on this exploration with me. It is with the hope that this book ignites your curiosity, expands your horizons, and encourages you to push the boundaries of knowledge.

- Aishwarya

ABOUT THE AUTHORS

Aishwarya Gupta is a dynamic leader with over two decades of industry experience in the Data and AI domain. Her expertise spans Strategy Consulting, Enterprise Transformation, Analyst Communications, Product & Program management, and she has a proven track record of driving remarkable business growth. With a strong customer-centric approach, she has successfully forged new partnerships, contributing to the acquisition of numerous high-profile clients during her previous role.

Notably, Aishwarya has played a pivotal role in championing diversity in leadership and mentoring women in the tech field. Her commitment to this cause led to her recognition and the prestigious "Best Firm in Women in Tech" award by Analytics India Magazine. Recognized as a thought leader, she was invited by IIT Madras to review their BS degree program in Data Science and Machine Learning. A prominent figure in the field, Aishwarya collaborates closely with premier educational institutions, driving efforts to bridge the skill gap between organizations and academia.

A published author, Aishwarya penned the "AI for Everyone" booklet, published by NASSCOM in Hindi, contributing to the dissemination of AI knowledge. She is an advocate for Adaptive AI adoption in its simplest form, and her influence extends to her role as a panelist in numerous AI external events. A contributor to AI trends reports, including those published by Pcloudy, Aishwarya continues to shape the discourse on emerging AI strategies.

Her commitment to sustainable practices is evident through her role as a brand ambassador for Waste Management & Plantation in Delhi NCR. Her impactful efforts were recognized when her guidance led to her community being honored as the first zero-waste society, acknowledged by the District Magistrate of Ghaziabad. Further, Aishwarya's dedication extends to her appointment as a Certified Mentor of Change by Niti Ayog, Govt of India, where she is involved in educating 2 lac girls under the STEM Initiative.

Beyond her professional accolades, Aishwarya's commitment to sustainability and community upliftment truly sets her apart. Her multifaceted contributions, from leadership in tech to environmental advocacy, embody a profound dedication to making a lasting impact.

ABOUT THE AUTHORS

Joseph Bulger has accumulated nearly 20 years of experience in engineering software systems across various industries. He has taken on multiple roles and successfully delivered diverse projects throughout his career.

Currently, Joseph holds the position of technical director at a media company that delivers content around the globe for some of the most recognizable brands in the industry. In this role, he has taken on the responsibility of guiding and mentoring multiple teams across a variety of areas.

As Joseph's focus shifts more towards leadership, he finds himself engaging in less hands-on engineering and development work. Instead, he devotes his time to leading his teams and imparting the knowledge and skills he has gained over the years.

As of late, Joseph has been spending more time researching ways that AI can play a role in accelerating the delivery of his teams as an addition tool in their toolbelt. Prompt engineering has become a recent topic within his space on how best it can be utilized as a productivity boost. Joseph hopes that through his shared experience others can see the potential in this exciting and quickly growing space.

ABOUT THE AUTHORS

Gaurav Aroraa is a Lead Architect at IBM with over 27 years of industry experience, encompassing a wide range of technologies. He has achieved notable accomplishments throughout his career, including being a MuleSoft Mentor, recipient of the Microsoft MVP award, and serving as a Mentor of Change with AIM NITI Aayog, Govt. of India. Gaurav is also a Business Coach with Business Blaster, Govt. of NCT of Delhi. He holds a lifetime membership with the Computer Society of India (CSI) and serves as an advisory member and Senior Mentor at India Mentor. He is certified as a Scrum trainer and Coach, ITIL-F certified, and holds PRINCE-F and PRINCE-P certifications. Additionally, he is a Certified Microsoft Azure Architect and has authored books on various technologies.

Gaurav recently achieved the distinction of being recognized as a World Record Holder for his exceptional book writing in technologies. He holds 15 patents in disciplined technologies. Gaurav is passionate about sharing his knowledge and believes in the principle of "sharing is caring". He actively mentors underprivileged students and is associated with the NGO SHIKSHA एक पहल.

ABOUT THE TECHNICAL REVIEWER

Pujarini Mohapatra is a seasoned professional with 15+ years of experience in Enterprise Software Services, Product Development & Management. With deep expertise in Enterprise Software and strategic product delivery, Pujarini has led large teams through dynamic business environments. She excels in managing complex programs, overseeing Product Development, and driving Customer Acquisition. Her domain spans Finance, Banking, Sales, Media, and robotic Process Automation.

She is the Principal Engineering Manager at Microsoft's Power Platform Customer Advisory Team. In her previous role, she worked as Associate Director at Novartis and co-founder at InteGen IT Services, Wells Fargo, Tech Mahindra, and Microsoft, showcasing her impact in architecture, automation, and leadership.

Pujarini holds an MCA from ICFAI University and completed the General Management Program at the Indian School of Business. Her passion for innovation and strategic leadership defines her journey. She can be reached at: https://linkedin.com/in/biswapm/

PREFACE

In the world of technology, innovation has always been the guiding star, illuminating new pathways and horizons that once seemed beyond our reach. As we stand at the threshold of a new era, an era where human ingenuity intertwines with the capabilities of machines, we find ourselves at the forefront of a monumental transformation – the age of Artificial Intelligence.

Welcome to "Exploring Generative AI: A Comprehensive Journey". Whether you are a novice taking your first steps into the world of AI or a seasoned professional navigating the complexities of the field, this book is designed to be your trusted companion, guiding you through the fascinating realm of Generative AI.

The current landscape is marked by the resounding crescendo of Generative AI, a phenomenon that has captivated both the tech industry and the collective imagination. The pages that follow uncover the intricate layers of Generative AI, charting its meteoric rise, its entwined destiny with real-world applications, and its transformative potential.

Our exploration ventures beyond the surface, delving into the foundations of Generative AI. We traverse through diverse models, dissecting their mechanics, and demystifying their underlying concepts. Through carefully crafted code examples, we bridge the gap between theory and practice, offering you a tangible grasp of these complex ideas.

However, this book is not confined to the realms of Generative AI alone. It is a holistic odyssey through the expansive universe of Artificial Intelligence. As AI continues to weave its tapestry across industries and sectors, our narrative unfolds to encompass broader vistas, highlighting the diverse landscapes of this dynamic field.

We extend our heartfelt gratitude to every reader, novice and expert alike, for joining us in this exploration. Your willingness to venture into the uncharted territories of AI reflects a spirit of curiosity and a commitment to progress. As we navigate through the intricacies of Generative AI and beyond, remember that you are not just reading a book – you are partaking in a transformative journey that has the potential to reshape our world.

Let us embark together on this odyssey of discovery, innovation, and limitless imagination.

What's Inside This Book

Chapter 1: Artificial Intelligence: an overview – provides a comprehensive introduction to the fundamentals of Artificial Intelligence, its historical context, and its evolution, setting the stage for deeper explorations in subsequent chapters.

Chapter 2: Understanding Generative AI: Core concepts - elucidates the core concepts, underlying principles, and different approaches involved in creating AI models that generate novel content.

Chapter 3: An Introduction to Prompt Engineering – introduces the art and science of crafting effective prompts to direct Generative AI models, shaping their outputs.

Chapter 4: Need of AI Models – examines the necessity and varied applications of AI models across industries, elucidating why they are essential components of modern technological landscapes.

Chapter 5: Content generation using Generative AI and its authenticity: delves into generating content using AI models while addressing concerns surrounding authenticity and verification.

Chapter 6: Ethical AI: discussion of Legal aspects on Generative AI– examines the implications, challenges, and legal frameworks governing its ethical use.

Chapter 7: Generative AI – as a threat to security – Highlighting potential security threats posed by Generative AI, this chapter analyzes the vulnerabilities and risks associated with the misuse of AI-generated content.

For Whom This Book Is Intended

This book is designed for:

- Novice enthusiasts seeking to explore Generative AI's potential.

- Industry Experts looking for real life applications of AI/Generative AI.

- Data scientists aiming to enhance their AI skill set.

- Tech innovators and entrepreneurs looking to integrate AI creatively.

- Professionals in diverse industries are eager to leverage AI-driven solutions.

- No prior AI experience required; basic programming knowledge beneficial.

Download the color images

For color images/diagrams/graphs used in the book, readers can download from: https://l1nk.dev/9788196612740.

Sharing Your Perspective and Providing Feedback

Your perspective is invaluable to us, as it helps us enhance our content and gather your feedback. We warmly welcome all forms of feedback. Please feel free to send us an email at feedback@arcchieonline.com, mentioning the book title in the subject line of your message.

Book Review Invitation

We kindly invite you to share your thoughts. After you've read and engaged with this book, consider leaving a review on the platform where you acquired it. Your impartial feedback can greatly assist potential readers in making informed decisions. Your reviews provide valuable insights for us at Arcchie, helping us better understand your perspectives on our products, and they offer authors the chance to appreciate your feedback on their work.

PIRACY

Should you encounter unauthorized reproductions of our publications in any digital format on the internet, we kindly request your assistance in pinpointing their locations or website sources. Please reach out to us at copyright@arcchieonline.com and include a link to the infringing material.

If you possess expertise in a particular subject and wish to participate in the creation or contribution to a book, please visit authors.arcchieonline.com. We welcome your exploration of authorship opportunities.

Chapter 1

Artificial Intelligence – an overview

Artificial Intelligence (AI) is booming everywhere. In this chapter, we will understand what Artificial Intelligence is all about.

The following topics will be covered in this chapter:

- What is Artificial Intelligence
- What is it not? How is it different from Automation
- The Evolution of Artificial Intelligence
- The ABC of Artificial Intelligence and its types
- Artificial Intelligence – The Mother – Rising with Generative AI

What is Artificial Intelligence

Artificial Intelligence (AI) is the ability of a computer or a robot controlled by a computer to do tasks that are usually done by humans because they require human intelligence and discernment. Although there are no AIs that can perform the wide variety of tasks an ordinary human can do, some AIs can match humans in specific tasks.

Artificial Intelligence is about decision-making for machines. Robotics is about putting computing in motion. And machine learning is about using data to make predictions about what might happen in the future or what the system ought to do.

What it is not

Human behavior is differentiated based on its intelligence, while even the most complicated animal/insect behavior is never taken as an indication of intelligence.

What is the difference?

- Consider the behavior of the digger wasp; when the female wasp returns to her burrow with food, she first deposits it on the threshold, checks for intruders inside her burrow, and only then, if the coast is clear, carries her food inside.
- The real nature of the wasp's instinctual behavior is revealed if the food is moved a few inches away from the entrance to her burrow while she is inside: on emerging, she will repeat the whole procedure as often as the food is displaced. Intelligence—conspicuously absent in the case of Wasp—must include the ability to adapt to new circumstances.

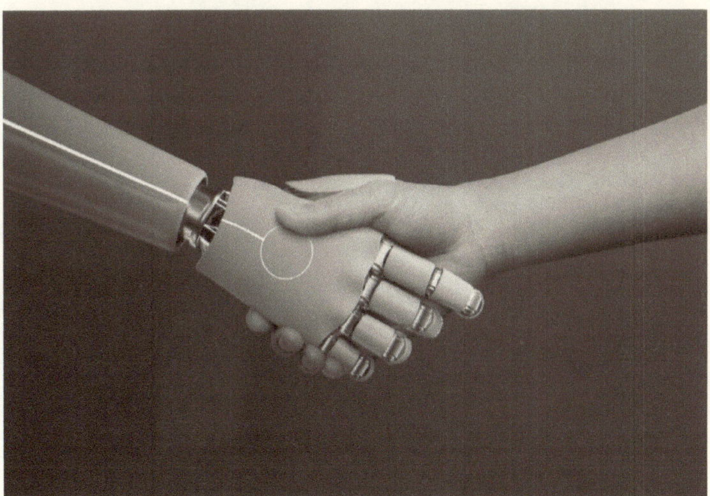

Figure 1.1: *Visualizing Human and AI Interacting Behavior*

Psychologists generally do not characterize human intelligence by just one characteristic but by the compilation of many diverse abilities. Research in AI has focused chiefly on the following components of intelligence: learning, reasoning, problem-solving, perception, language, the art of communication, and most importantly, empathy and the ability to THINK.

Human Intelligence alludes to people's scholarly ability that permits us to think, gain from various expressions, comprehend complex ideas, solve numerical issues, adapt to new situations, use knowledge to manipulate one's environment, and speak with fellow human beings. What makes human intelligence remarkable is that it is supported by conceptual feelings such as energy and inspiration that empower people to achieve complex psychological assignments.

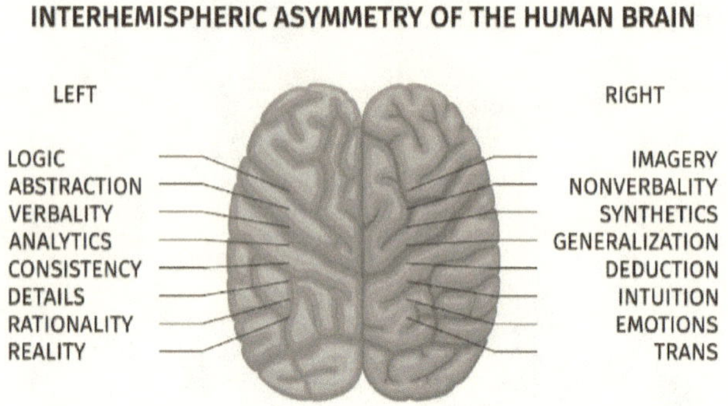

INTERHEMISPHERIC ASYMMETRY OF THE HUMAN BRAIN

LEFT

RIGHT

LOGIC
ABSTRACTION
VERBALITY
ANALYTICS
CONSISTENCY
DETAILS
RATIONALITY
REALITY

IMAGERY
NONVERBALITY
SYNTHETICS
GENERALIZATION
DEDUCTION
INTUITION
EMOTIONS
TRANS

Figure 1.2: Visualizing Types of Human Intelligence

Human intelligence is the thing that shapes the development and appropriation of man-made consciousness and creative arrangements related to it. It is human intelligence that tries to ask 'why' and considers 'imagine a scenario where' through basic reasoning. As engineering design keeps on being tested by complex issues and the nature of information, the requirement for human oversight, skill, and quality affirmation is basic in using AI-created yields.

What are the limitations of human intelligence?

Human intelligence is a term for the cognitive capabilities of humans, including their reasoning and problem-solving skills. There are many limitations to human intelligence, such as only being able to process a limited amount of information in a given time period, having limited memories and self-control, and being prone to errors when processing complex tasks.

Each of these limitations has a corresponding limit to the amount of information that can be processed in a given time period. For example, a person can only hold a limited amount of information in their short-term memory. This means that they are not able to retain more information than they can process in a short period of time. Memory is a cognitive process that allows humans to remember and recall past experiences. Memory is encoded in the brain in the form of neural structures and can be accessed through thought or re-collective activity. Memory is affected by a variety of factors, including age, education, and experience.

Some of the further main limitations of human intelligence include cognitive biases, limited attention span, and poor problem-solving skills. Cognitive biases are tendencies to believe or perceive things in certain ways. These biases can cause us to make decisions that may not be based on logic and reason. Lack of attention is another limitation of human intelligence. We can only process a limited amount of information at one time. We rely on intuition and emotions more than logic when making decisions. And we have cognitive biases that influence how we process information. This leads to poor problem-solving skills. We may not recognize a problem, or if we do, we may not know how to solve it. Also, our emotions can cloud our judgment.

So how do we solve problems? We use heuristics. Heuristics are mental shortcuts that help us make decisions quickly and easily. They are based on past experiences or rules of thumb. We use heuristics to make decisions about whether or not we should purchase something, how long it will take us to complete a task, and even if we like someone.

Heuristics can be helpful, but they can also lead to errors in judgment.

So if we look at the above traits, AI is not intelligence—it is a prediction. With large language models, we've seen an increase in the machine's ability to accurately predict and execute a desired outcome. But it would be a mistake to equate this to human intelligence.

Artificial intelligence advancements are built by numerical cycles that influence expanding figuring capacity to convey quicker and more precise models and estimates of operational systems or upgraded portrayals and blends of huge data sets. Nevertheless, while these trendsetting innovations can play out certain assignments with higher productivity and precision, human ability assumes a basic part in planning and using AI innovation.

AI is rising very quickly, and it is encouraging human beings to become more productive and live a reasonable life.

Evolution of Artificial Intelligence

The evolution of Artificial Intelligence (AI) is a fascinating journey that spans several decades. Here's a high-level overview of the key milestones and developments in the field of AI:

1. Early Foundations (1950s-1960s):
    - The term "Artificial Intelligence" was coined by John McCarthy in 1956.
    - Researchers began developing the first AI programs, including the Logic Theorist and General Problem Solver.
    - The focus was on symbolic AI, which used rules and logic to solve problems.
2. AI Winter (1970s-1980s):
    - Progress in AI research slowed down due to over-optimistic expectations and lack of computational power.
    - Funding for AI research decreased, leading to a period known as the "AI winter."
3. Expert Systems (1980s):
    - Expert systems, which encoded human knowledge and reasoning into computer programs, gained popularity.
    - Dendral, MYCIN, and other expert systems demonstrated the potential of AI in specialized domains.
4. Machine Learning Resurgence (1990s):
    - Machine learning techniques, such as neural networks and decision trees, started to gain traction.
    - AI research began to shift towards practical applications in fields like natural language processing and computer vision.
5. Rise of Big Data (2000s):
    - The availability of large datasets and improved algorithms led to significant advancements in AI.
    - Technologies like support vector machines and deep

      learning became more prominent.

6. Deep Learning and Neural Networks (2010s):
   - Deep learning, particularly deep neural networks, revolutionized AI.
   - Breakthroughs in image and speech recognition, as well as the success of deep learning in competitions like ImageNet, attracted significant attention.
7. AI in Everyday Life (2010s-2020s):
   - AI applications became ubiquitous, from virtual assistants like Siri and Alexa to recommendation systems, autonomous vehicles, and healthcare diagnostics.
   - AI also made inroads in industries like finance, marketing, and manufacturing.
8. Ethical and Societal Concerns (2010s-Present):
   - The growing impact of AI on society raised concerns about bias, privacy, and job displacement.
   - Ethical considerations and regulations, like GDPR, started to shape AI development.
9. Advancements in Reinforcement Learning (2010s-Present):
   - Reinforcement learning gained popularity, leading to achievements in areas like game playing (e.g., Alpha-Go) and robotics.
10. AI for Healthcare and Biotechnology (2020s):
    - AI made significant contributions to drug discovery, medical diagnostics, and genomics.
11. AI and Automation (2020s-Present):
    - The integration of AI in various industries led to discussions about the future of work and the need for reskilling.
12. Quantum Computing and AI (ongoing):
    - Research into the potential of quantum computing to accelerate AI computations is ongoing.
13. AI Safety and Ethics (ongoing):
    - Research and development in AI ethics, fairness, and safety are increasingly important.

The evolution of AI is marked by periods of optimism and disappointment, but in recent years, AI has made tremendous strides and is becoming an integral part of modern life. Its applications continue to expand across various domains, and the field continues to evolve, driven by advances in technology and growing societal awareness of its potential benefits and challenges.

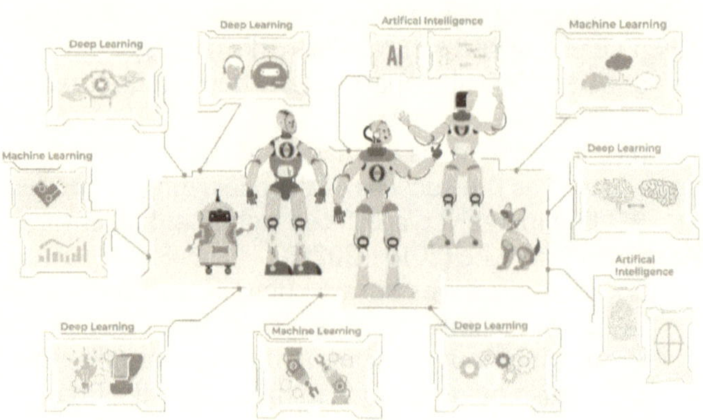

Figure 1.3: *Evolution of Artificial Intelligence*

Following are the fundamental differences between artificial intelligence and human intelligence:

- If we can compare it to nature wise, then human intelligence intends to revise to modern environments by using a mixture of distinct cognitive procedures, whereas artificial intelligence intends to create devices that can mock human behavior and conduct human-like actions. Thus, we can say that the human brain is analogous, but machines are digital.
- The simple difference is that human beings use their brain, ability to think, and memory, while AI machines depend on the data given to them.
- As we all know that humans learn from past mistakes, and intelligent ideas and intelligent attitudes lie at the basis of human intelligence. Hence, this point is simply because machines cannot think and learn from the past. They can learn from information and through regular training, but they can never attain the thinking procedure unique to humans.
- Artificial intelligence takes much more time to adjust to new changes, whereas human beings can adapt to changes easily, and this makes people able to learn and ace several abilities.
- Modern computers normally use 2 watts of energy, whereas human brains use about 25 watts.
- Machines can handle more data at a speedier rate as compared to humans. As of now, humans cannot beat the speed

of computers.
- Artificial Intelligence has not aced the ability to choose related social and excited codes. People are many ways better at social interaction since they can develop academic data, have self-awareness, and are elegant to others' emotions.

Artificial Intelligence has come a long way from being a component of science fiction to reality, and there is no doubt that artificial intelligence is shaping every industry and taking the world to the next level.

But it is still not possible to exactly mimic the level of human intelligence. Computers cannot copy the thought process of humans, and according to experts, it won't be possible in the coming future. Since scientists and experimenters still don't know the maze behind the human thought procedure. It is highly uncertain that we will generate machines that can think like humans anytime soon.

Similarities between Human Intelligence and Artificial Intelligence

There are many similarities between Human Intelligence and Artificial Intelligence. They both can process data, learn, and reason. In addition, they share the same goal of achieving success in various tasks.

What tasks are easier for Humans or Artificial Intelligence?

- Artificial intelligence is better at certain types of tasks than humans, but it's not as good at other types of tasks.
- Tasks that are easier for artificial intelligence include tasks that require simple rules and calculations.
- Tasks that are easier for humans include tasks that require thinking, creativity, and critical thinking.

What are the benefits and drawbacks of Human Intelligence vs. Artificial Intelligence?

- Artificial Intelligence has a lot of potential advantages over human intelligence in terms of tasks that it can complete faster and more accurately than humans can. For example, AI systems are able to quickly learn new tasks by trial and error rather than needing instruction manuals or feedback from humans.

They're also better at understanding complex patterns or structures than humans are- which could be useful for areas like finance or medicine, where accuracy is important. However, artificial intelligence doesn't have the same flexibility as human intelligence when it comes to thinking outside the box or improvising on the spot- two skills that come in handy for many jobs.

In addition, while AI systems are getting better at recognizing emotions in photos and videos- something that's currently difficult for computers to do- we don't yet know what kind of ethical implications this will have in the future.

Strengths & Weaknesses of Human Intelligence and Artificial Intelligence

In this section, we will discuss the Strengths and Weaknesses of Human Intelligence and Artificial Intelligence.

Strengths of Human Intelligence

- Human intelligence is the only type of intelligence that can be improved over time.
- Humans are creative and intuitive problem solvers.
- People with high human intelligence can learn quickly and retain information better than people with low human intelligence.
- People with high human intelligence are better at recognizing patterns than those with low human intelligence.

Weaknesses of Human Intelligence

There are weaknesses in human intelligence that can be exploited by computers.

Some of these weaknesses include:

Limited understanding of complex situations and problems.

- Inability to reason abstractly.
- Lack of creativity and innovation.
- Problem-solving skills.

Strengths of Artificial Intelligence

Artificial Intelligence (AI) is a field of computer science that deals with the design and development of intelligent agents, which are systems that can act autonomously.

There are many strengths to AI, including:

- Artificial intelligence can help us automate tasks and processes.
- It is able to learn from data and improve over time.
- It can create complex models for understanding complex systems.
- AI can provide insights that humans cannot access on their own.

Weakness of Artificial Intelligence

Artificial intelligence (AI) is a field of computer science and engineering that deals with the creation of intelligent agents, which are programs designed to simulate or emulate human behavior. AI has been used in many different fields, including business, finance, healthcare, marketing, and search engine optimization (SEO). However, there are some potential weaknesses of AI. For example, AI can sometimes be inaccurate or vulnerable to simple tricks. Additionally, because AI relies on data input from humans for training and feedback loops during learning processes may not always work as intended due to human biases and errors. As such, there is still some way to go before artificial intelligence becomes truly reliable and effective in all situations.

Figure **1.4**: *Visualizing Human and Artificial Intelligence Mindset*

The two terms are often used interchangeably, but there are important differences between them. Human intelligence refers to the cognitive abilities of humans, while artificial intelligence (AI) refers to any system that performs tasks that would traditionally be considered within the capability or realm of the human intellect, such as reasoning, problem-solving, and decision-making under controlled conditions.

```
TIP: The development of full artificial intelligence could spell
the end of the human race…. It would take off on its own and re-
design itself at an ever-increasing rate. Humans, who are limited
by slow biological evolution, couldn't compete and would be
superseded."- Stephen Hawking, BBC
```

Automation Vs. Artificial Intelligence

Automation and AI are often used interchangeably, but they are very different.

Automation: Automation is a process that executes itself with little or no human interaction by some specific patterns and rules to perform repetitive tasks. Automation is widely used in E-Commerce, Banking, and the Telecommunication industry, like automated customer self-service for booking any kind of appointment or ticket these days.

Artificial Intelligence: Artificial Intelligence (AI) is a branch of computer science that creates intelligent machines that can work and react like humans. It can be defined as the collection of different technologies that allow the machine to act at the human level of intelligence. This process requires learning from past experiences and self-correction to make a certain decision and to reach a certain conclusion.

Sl. No.	Artificial Intelligence	Automation
1.	AI makes a decision based on the learning from experience & information it receives.	Automation is like pre-set and self-running to perform specific tasks.
2.	AI is a system that helps experts to analyze situations and arrive at a certain conclusion	Automation is a kind of machine programmed to carry out a routine job
3.	AI is for non-repetitive tasks.	While Automation is for repetitive tasks based on commands and rules
4.	AI involves learning and evolving	Automation does not involve learning and evolving
5.	AI interacts with humans; it learns from experience and compares the situations, and then works according to them	While Automation has no interaction with humans, and it works on instructions
6.	It is possible for AI systems to "understand" data.	An automated system collects data.

7.	A computer is capable of thinking on its own once it has learned how to perform every AI activity. To exemplify, Amazon selects the item most suitable to your taste from its million products based on what the system thinks would be the best course of action	It follows your instructions exactly; no decisions are made by it.

Table 1.1: Artificial Intelligence vs Automation

ABC of Artificial intelligence

As Stephen Hawking had clearly projected, "AI is humanity's gigantic step into a robotic future. It can design improvements to itself and conquer mankind before we know it. But before we bow down to the will of robots, we need to know how they are constructed.

If it interests you, you must watch "Theory of Everything," a movie on Stephen Hawking's life, and the movie on Alan Turing " The Imitation Game" -The Imitation Game is a 2014 American period biographical thriller film directed by Morten Tyldum and written by Graham Moore, based on the 1983 biography Alan Turing: The Enigma by Andrew Hodges. The film's title quotes the name of the game cryptanalyst Alan Turing proposed to answer the question "Can machines think?" in his 1950 seminal paper "Computing Machinery and Intelligence."

Nowadays, we are not surprised to find personalized advertising when browsing the Internet or receive recommendations for audiovisual content from streaming platforms that seem made by someone who knows us better than we know ourselves. However, the potential of artificial intelligence (AI) responsible for these situations goes far beyond that. In the current COVID-19 pandemic, for example, it has been used to predict the number of ICU beds required, as well as in applications offering rapid disease diagnoses by means of X-ray analyses. Health, education, mobility, banking, insurance... Although this technology is at its height nowadays, its development has been ongoing for decades, and it can now offer solutions in almost every aspect of our lives.

Sometimes without even being aware of it, artificial intelligence has a constant presence in our everyday lives. In part, it is responsible for helping us reach our destination on time when we search for an optimum route on our GPS or for our smartphone sorting photos by places, themes, or people without having to label them. AI is also behind a conversational assistant fulfilling our commands when we ask for the lights or music to be turned on, or telling us the latest news or the traffic we may encounter on our way to work, and our email provider filtering out messages that may be spam; or social networks suggesting new friends

It's the Algorithm: That brings Magic

Although we may feel it is very modern, artificial intelligence emerged in the 1950s as a branch of computer science. Specifically, the term was coined in 1956 during a meeting of experts in information theory, neural networks, computing, abstraction, and creativity at the University of Dartmouth (USA). More than a technology in itself, as we will see, AI is actually a myriad of technologies that seek to enable machines to perceive, understand, act, and learn. This discipline, therefore, strives to develop computer systems capable of performing tasks normally attributed to human intelligence, such as recognizing objects, identifying faces, driving vehicles, detecting diseases, or understanding natural language, both spoken and written. There could possibly be thousands more, almost as many as the tasks we perform in our daily lives. Algorithms play a key role in all of them.

An algorithm is an ordered set of instructions, operations, steps, or processes that enable a particular task to be completed or a solution to be found when some problem arises. We could say that it is like a list of preset instructions that guide the decisions to be made. For example, bring a vehicle to a halt at a STOP sign. Algorithms are the essence of any artificial intelligence system and are trained by providing them with as much data as possible to act as references so that they can learn more and progress. Have you ever accessed the photo gallery on your smartphone and seen a message asking you to confirm who the person in the picture is? That has a lot to do with what we are talking about here. In such a case, the device is asking you for help to compile more information and improve its face identification skills. By fine-tuning its classification, the next time you want to search for photos of a relative, you will simply have to type in their name, and your smartphone will be able to retrieve everything associated with that person in under a second.

Let's go Deeper! The Types of AI

Artificial Intelligence (AI) can be categorized into several types based on its capabilities, functionalities, and the extent to which it can replicate human intelligence. Here are some of the primary types of AI:

- **Narrow or Weak AI (ANI)**: Narrow AI is designed for a specific task or a limited set of tasks. It operates within a predefined range of functions and lacks general intelligence. Examples include virtual assistants like Siri and Alexa, chatbots, and recommendation systems.
- **General or Strong AI (AGI)**: General AI possesses human-like intelligence and can understand, learn, and apply knowledge across a wide range of tasks. It can perform any intellectual task that a human can do. The development of AGI is still largely theoretical and remains a subject of ongoing research.
- **Artificial Narrow General Intelligence (ANGI)**: ANGI is an intermediary concept that combines elements of both narrow and general AI. It can perform specific tasks but is also capable of transferring knowledge and skills between tasks. ANGI exhibits some degree of learning and adaptability across multiple domains.
- **Machine Learning (ML)**: Machine learning is a subset of AI that focuses on developing algorithms that can learn from data. It includes supervised learning, unsupervised learning, and reinforcement learning. ML is used in various applications like image recognition, natural language processing, and predictive analytics.
- **Deep Learning (DL)**: Deep learning is a subset of machine

learning that uses neural networks with multiple layers to model and process complex data. It's particularly effective for tasks like image and speech recognition. DL has revolutionized AI by enabling it to perform more human-like tasks.

- **Reinforcement Learning (RL)**: Reinforcement learning is a type of machine learning where an agent learns to make sequences of decisions to maximize a cumulative reward. It is often used in robotics, gaming, and autonomous systems.
- **Natural Language Processing (NLP)**: NLP is a specialized field within AI that focuses on enabling machines to understand, interpret, and generate human language. It's used in chatbots, language translation, sentiment analysis, and more.
- **Computer Vision (CV)**: Computer vision enables machines to interpret and understand visual information from the world, such as images and videos. Applications include facial recognition, object detection, and autonomous vehicles.
- **Expert Systems**: Expert systems are designed to mimic the decision-making abilities of a human expert in a specific domain. They use knowledge bases and inference engines to make recommendations or solve problems within that domain.
- **Robotics AI**: Robotics AI involves the use of AI in controlling and enhancing the capabilities of robots. It's used in industries like manufacturing, healthcare, and space exploration.
- **Emotion AI**: Emotion AI, also known as Affective Computing, focuses on recognizing and responding to human emotions. It's used in applications like sentiment analysis, affective computing, and emotional chatbots.
- **Autonomous AI**: Autonomous AI systems are capable of operating independently and making decisions without human intervention.

Examples include self-driving cars and drones.

These categories represent different aspects of AI, and many AI systems and applications may incorporate a combination of these types to achieve their goals. AI is a dynamic and evolving field, with ongoing research and developments continually expanding the scope of what AI can achieve.

Conclusion

Understanding the training process and architecture of ChatGPT provides insights into how the model is developed and how it generates text. It is a remarkable example of how transformer-based language models have revolutionized natural language processing tasks, including conversational AI.

In the next chapter, you will read various aspects related to language models, natural language processing (NLP), and conversational AI, followed by deep diving into generative AI concepts, fine-tuning language models, and Building Chatbots.

In next Chapter we will cover:

- Generative AI Introduction & Evolution
- How it's different from AI
- Core Concept of Generative AI

Chapter 2

Understanding Generative AI Core Concepts

Generative AI is subset of artificial intelligence that aims to generate new, original content that is indistinguishable from human-created data. It involves creating models that can learn the underlying patterns and structures of a given dataset and use that knowledge to produce new instances that are similar in nature. Generative AI allows machines to move beyond mere analysis and into the realm of creativity.

The following topics will be covered in this chapter:

- 1. Generative AI Introduction & Evolution
- 2. How it's different from AI
- 3. Core Concept of Generative AI
- 4. Generative AI Models and their usage
- 5. Generative AI application in the business world

History of Generative Artificial Intelligence (AI)

In 2023, generative AI became widely accessible. Users use GPT to accelerate a wide range of tasks, such as explaining concepts, summarizing or translating text, suggesting solutions for described problems, providing code snippets, and more.

In this book, my goal is to evangelize the main concept of generative AI without diving deep into technical details.

Generative AI is a type of Machine Learning - ML which, in general, aims to create models able to produce outputs based on data used in the training phase.

With traditional machine learning problems, the model output is one feature, either numerical or categorical. On the other hand, generative AI concern is to randomly create a new observation x that seems as if it was part of the initial training data set.

The field of Generative AI has witnessed remarkable advancements in the recent years. We believe there are three breakthrough moments in shaping today's generative AI; Generative Adversarial Networks (GAN) by I. Goodfellow et al. in 2014, Transformer models in 2017, and Reinforcement Learning with Human Feedback (RLHF) in the same year. Accompanied by these algorithmic strides, the continuous improvement of hardware acceleration has unlocked unprecedented capabilities, empowering the training of Large Language Models (LLMs) on colossal natural language datasets. However, the true turning point came with OpenAI's game-changing release of ChatGPT. This momentous launch, followed by the announcement of GPT3.5 and DALL-E 2 models on Azure, Google Bard, GPT4, and Microsoft CoPilot, ignited a wildfire of interest that has rapidly intensified, shaping the landscape of Generative AI in an exponential manner.

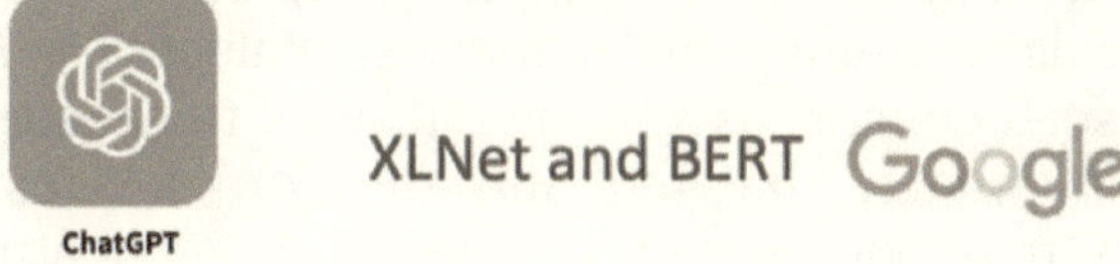

Figure 2.1: *Evolving AI*

The difference between AI and Generative AI

AI is the concept of endowing machines with the ability to exhibit intelligence. While it doesn't necessarily imply human-level intellect, it encompasses learning, planning, and problem-solving capacity. When AI is applied to specific tasks, it is known as **Artificial Narrow Intelligence (ANI)**. On the other hand, **Artificial General Intelligence (AGI)** aims to enable machines to utilize these capabilities for any cognitive task that humans can effortlessly perform, such as discerning a novel genre or piloting an aircraft. AGI is the ultimate realization of AI as it encompasses functions that the human brain can accomplish.

Over the years, Artificial Intelligence has made significant advancements since it was first coined by John McCarthy in 1956. Initially defined as the ability of a machine to perform tasks requiring human-like Intelligence, AI has evolved to encompass AGI, which represents the next level of AI development. While current AI technologies excel in predefined tasks, AGI aims to enable machines to learn independently and determine how to achieve any given goal.

Artificial Neural Networks, inspired by biological neural

networks, serve as an example of AGI. They solve complex problems in areas like vision and speech recognition, pushing the boundaries of AI. Artificial intelligence finds applications in various fields, including mathematics, philosophy, linguistics, cognitive science, and psychology. It aims to create machines that mimic human thinking and develop devices that can learn with minimal human intervention, replicating human information processing.

AGI refers to a goal-oriented system or an intelligent agent capable of autonomous operation, reducing the need for direct human supervision. AGI involves AI's independent development of technology to fulfill its designated purpose. It considers all available information to make decisions rather than being limited to specific situations.

It is crucial to emphasize that Artificial Intelligence and Artificial General Intelligence are not interchangeable terms. AI refers explicitly to machines that think like humans, while AGI focuses on providing AI systems with abstract goals applicable across various situations, aiming for broader capabilities.

Let's understand the core concepts

Let's provide a bit of context. So two very common questions asked are what is artificial intelligence, and what is the difference between AI and machine learning? One way to think about it is that AI is a discipline like physics, for example. AI is a branch of computer science that deals with the creation of intelligent agents, which are systems that can reason and learn and act autonomously. Essentially, AI has to do with the theory and methods to build machines that think and act like humans. In this discipline, we have machine learning, which is a subfield of AI. It is a program or system that trains a model from input data. The trained model can make useful predictions from new or never before seen data drawn from the same one used to train the model. Machine learning gives the computer the ability to learn without explicit programming. Two of the most common classes of machine learning models are unsupervised and supervised ML models.

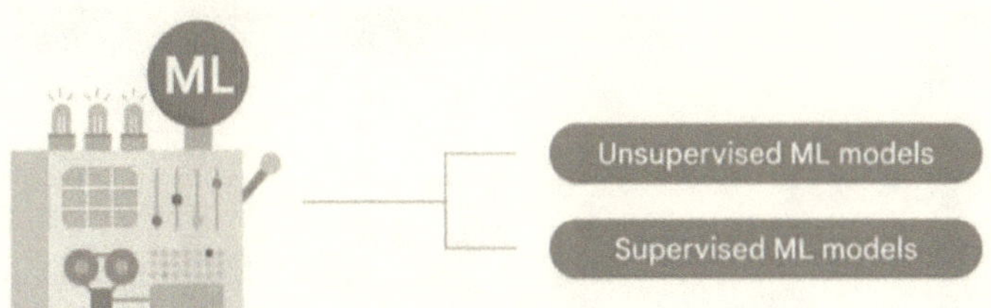

Figure 2.2: *Common Classes of ML model*

The key difference between the two is that with supervised models; we have labels. Labeled data is data that comes with a tag like a name, a type, or a number. Unlabelled data is data that comes with no tag. This graph is an example of the sort of problem that a supervised model might try to solve. For example, let's say you are the owner of a restaurant. You have historical data of the bill amount and how much different people tipped based on order type, whether it was picked up or delivered. In supervised Learning, the model learns from past examples to predict future values and, in this case, tips. So here, the model uses the total bill amount to predict the future tip amount based on whether an order was picked up or delivered.

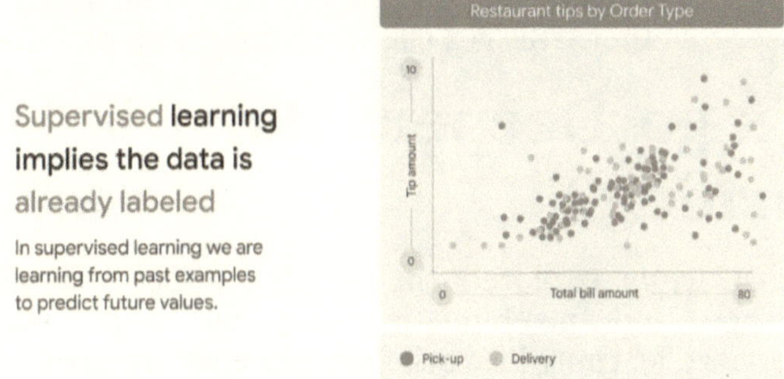

Figure 2.3: *Visualizing supervised learning data*

This is an example of the sort of problem that an unsupervised model might try to solve. So here you want to look at tenure and income and then group or cluster employees to see whether someone is on the fast track.

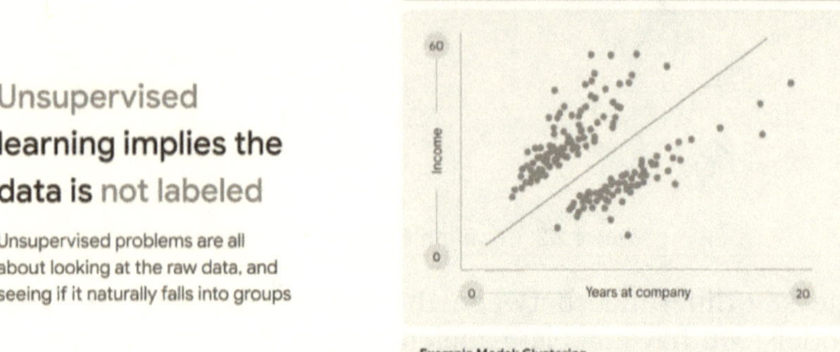

Figure 2.4: *Visualizing Unsupervised Learning Data*

Unsupervised problems are all about discovery, about looking at the raw data and seeing if it naturally falls into groups. Let's get a little deeper and show this graphically. As understanding these concepts is the foundation for your understanding of generative AI. In supervised learning testing, data values or x are input into the model. The model outputs a prediction and compares that prediction to the training data used to train the model. If the predicted test data values and actual training data values are far apart. Then this is called an error, and the model tries to reduce this error until the predicted and actual values are closer together. This is a classic optimization problem.

Let's go Deeper! What is Deep Learning?

Now that we've explored the difference between artificial intelligence and machine learning and supervised and unsupervised learning let's briefly explore where deep learning fits as a subset of machine learning methods.

While machine learning is a broad field that encompasses many different techniques.

Deep learning is a type of machine learning that uses artificial neural networks, allowing them to process more complex patterns than machine learning. Artificial neural networks are inspired by the human brain. They are made up of many interconnected nodes or neurons that can learn to perform tasks by processing data and making predictions. Deep learning models typically have many layers of neurons, which allows them to learn more complex patterns than traditional machine learning models. And neural networks can use both labeled and unlabelled data. This is called semi-supervised learning. In semi-supervised learning, a neural network is trained on a small amount of labeled data and a large amount of unlabelled data. The labeled data helps the neural network to learn the basic concepts of the task, while the unlabelled data helps the neural network to generalize to new examples. Now we finally get to where generative AI fits into this AI discipline.

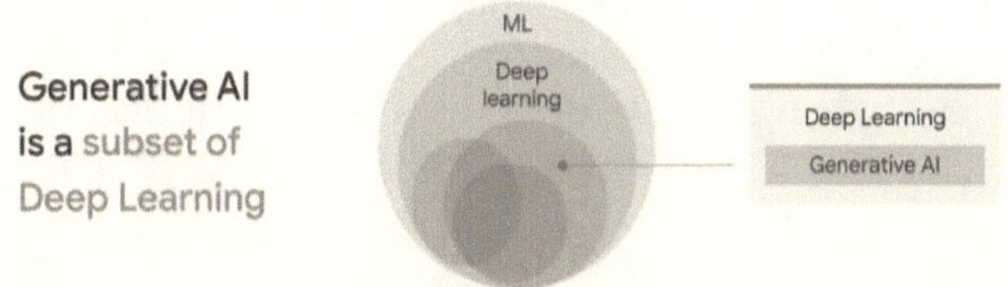

Figure 2.5: *Gen AI is a subset of Deep Learning*

This means it uses artificial neural networks and can process both labeled and unlabeled data using supervised, unsupervised, and semi-supervised methods. Large language models are also a subset of deep learning. Deep learning models, or machine learning models in general, can be divided into two types generative and discriminative. A discriminative model is a type of model that is used to classify or predict labels for data points. Discriminative models are typically trained on a data set of labelled data points and they learn the relationship between the features of the data points and the labels. Once a discriminative model is trained, it can be used to predict the label for new data points. A generative model generates new data instances based on a learned probability distribution of existing data. Thus, generative models generate new content.

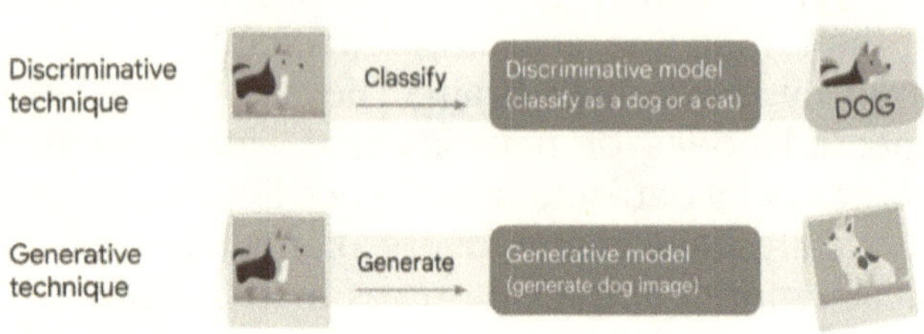

Figure 2. 6: *Generative techniques*

Take this example: The discriminative model learns the conditional probability distribution or the probability of y our output given x our input that this is a dog and classifies it as a dog and not a cat. The generative model learns the joint probability distribution or the probability of x and y and predicts the conditional probability that this is a dog and can then generate a picture of a dog. So, to summarize, generative models can generate new data instances while discriminative models discriminate between different kinds of data instances.

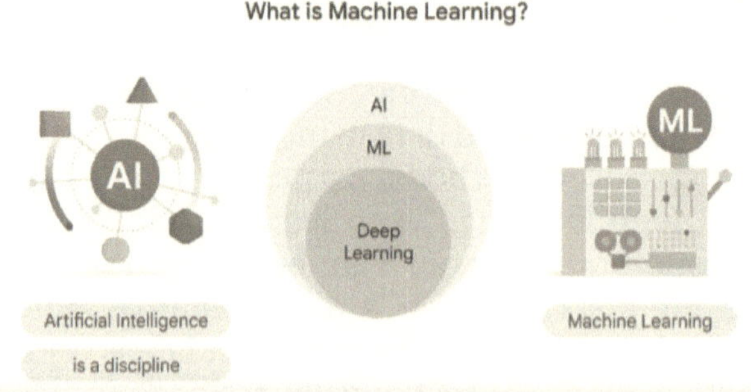

Figure 2.7: *Machine Learning*

The preceding `Figure 2.7` shows a traditional machine learning model which attempts to learn the relationship between the data and the label or what you want to predict. The bottom image shows a generative AI model which attempts to learn patterns on content so that it can generate new content. A good way to distinguish what is GenAI and what is not is shown in this illustration. It is not GenAI when the output or y or label is a number or a class. For example, spam or not spam or a probability.

What Else is GENERATIVE AI?

It is GenAI when the output is natural language like speech or text, an image or audio, for example. Visualizing this mathematically would look like this; if you haven't seen this for a while, the y is equal to the f(x) equation, which calculates the dependent output of a process given different inputs. The y stands for the model output, the f embodies the function used in the calculation, and the x represents the input or inputs used for the formula. So the model output is a function of all the inputs. If y is a number like predicted sales, it is not GenAI; if y is a sentence like defined sales, it is generative. As the question would elicit a text response, the response would be based on all the massive large data the model was already trained on.

It's been shown and created something entirely new based on that information. Large language models are one type of generative AI since they generate novel combinations of text in the form of natural-sounding language. A generative image model takes an image as input and can output text, another image, or video. For example, under the output text, you can get visual question answering, while under output image, an image completion is generated, and under output, video animation is generated. A generative language model takes text as input and can output more text, an image, audio, or decisions. For example, under the output text, question answering is generated, and under the output image, a video is generated. We've stated that generative language models learn about patterns in language through training data, then, given some text, they predict what comes next. Thus, generative language models are pattern-matching systems; they learn about patterns based on the data you provide.

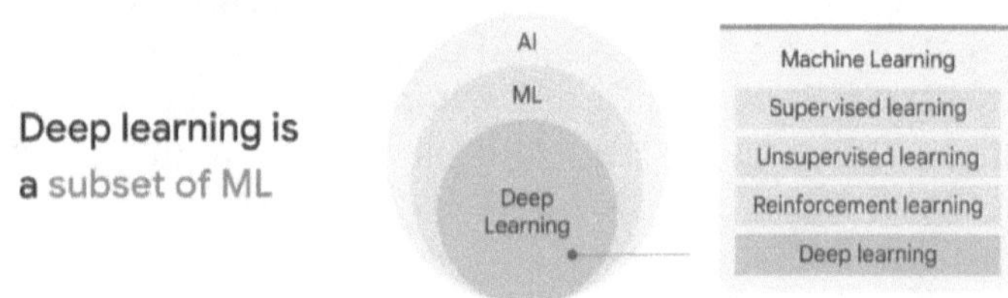

Figure 2.8: *Deep Learning is a subset of ML*

Here is an example; based on things it learned from its training data, it offers predictions of how to complete this sentence, I'm making a sandwich with peanut butter and jelly. Here is the same example using Bard, which is trained on a massive amount of text data and is able to communicate and generate humanlike text in response to a wide range of prompts and questions. Here is another example, the meaning of life is, and Bard gives you a contextual answer and then shows the highest probability response. The power of generative AI comes from the use of transformers; transformers produced the 2018 revolution in natural language processing.

Types of models

At a high level, a transformer model consists of an encoder and a decoder; the encoder encodes the input sequence and passes

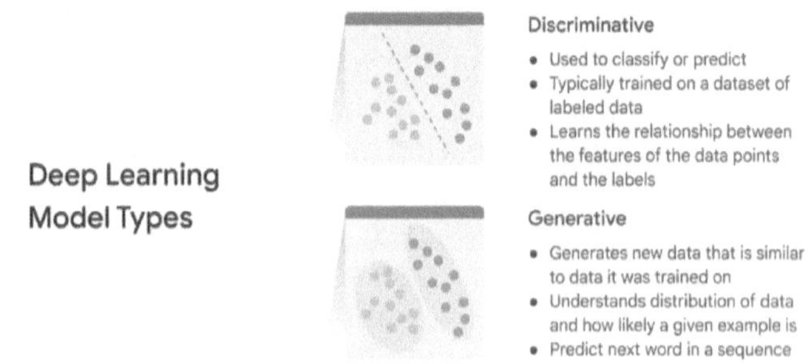

Figure 2.9: *Deep Learning – Model Types*

it to the decoder, which learns how to decode the representation for a relevant task. In transformers, hallucinations are words or phrases that are generated by the model that are often nonsensical or grammatically incorrect. Hallucinations can be caused by a number of factors, including the model is not trained on enough data. Or the model is trained on noisy or dirty data, or the model is not given enough context, or the model is not given enough constraints. Hallucinations can be a problem for transformers because they can make the output text difficult to understand. They can also make the model more likely to generate incorrect or misleading information. A prompt is a short piece of text that is given to the large language model as input, and it can be used to control the output of the model in a variety of ways. Prompt design is the process of creating a prompt that will generate the desired output from a large language model. As previously mentioned, GenAI depends a lot on the training data that you have fed into it, and it analyzes the patterns and structures of the input data and thus learns. But with access to a browser-based prompt, you, the user, can generate your own content.

Here are the associated model types, text-to-text. Well, text-to-text models take a natural language input and produce a text output; these models are trained to learn the mapping between a pair of text, for example, translation from one language to another. Text-to-image text-to-image models are trained on a large set of images. Each is captioned with a short text description. Diffusion is one method used to achieve this. Text-to-video and text-to-3D. Text-to-video models aim to generate a video representation from text input. The input text can be anything from a single sentence to a full script, and the output is a video that corresponds to the input text. Similarly, Text-to-3D models generate three-dimensional objects that correspond to a user's text description; for example, this can be used in games or other 3D worlds. Text-to-task. Text-to-task models are trained to perform a defined task or action based on text input. This task can be a wide range of actions, such as answering a question, performing a search, making a prediction, or taking some sort of action. For example, a text-to-task model could be trained to navigate web UI or make changes to a doc through the GUI. A foundation model is a large AI model pre-trained on a vast quantity of data designed to be adapted or fine-tuned to a wide range of downstream tasks such as sentiment analysis, image captioning, and object recognition. Foundation models have the potential to revolutionize many industries, including healthcare, finance, and customer service. They can be used to detect fraud and provide personalized customer support. Vertex AI offers a model garden that includes foundation models. The language foundation models include PaLM API for chat and text. The vision foundation models include stable diffusion, which has been shown to be effective at generating high-quality images from text descriptions. Let's say you have a use case where you need to gather sentiments about how your customers are feeling about your product or service. You can use the classification task, sentiment analysis task model for just that purpose. And what if you needed to perform occupancy analytics? There is a task model for your use case. Shown here are GenAI applications. Let's look at an example of code generation shown in the second block under code at the top. In this example, I've input a code file conversion problem converting from Python to JSON. I use Bard, and I insert into the prompt box the following.

I have a Pandas DataFrame with two columns, one with the file name and one with the hour in which it is generated. I'm trying to convert this into a JSON file in the format shown on screen. Bard returns the steps I need to do this and the code snippet. And here, my output is in a JSON format. It gets better. I happen to be using Google's free browser-based Jupyter Notebook, known as Colab, and I simply export the Python code to Google's Colab.

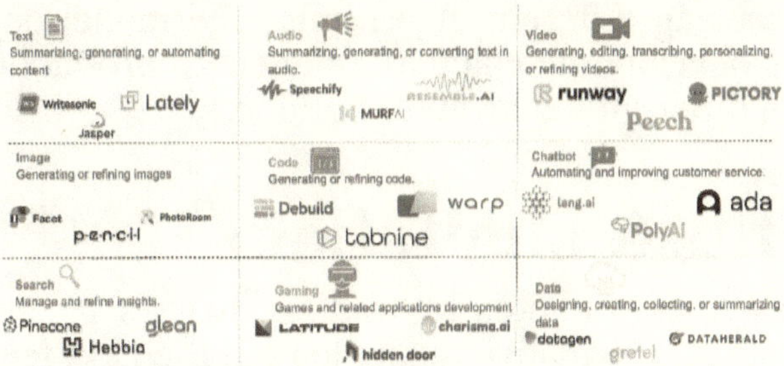

Figure 2.10: *Current Gen AI Landscape*

To summarize, Bard code generation can help you debug your lines of source code, explain your code to you line by line, craft SQL queries for your database, translate code from one language to another, and generate documentation and tutorials for source code. Generative AI Studio lets you quickly explore and customize GenAI models that you can leverage in your applications on Google Cloud. Generative AI Studio helps developers create and deploy GenAI models by providing a variety of tools and resources that make it easy to get started. For example, there is a library of pre-trained models, there is a tool for fine-tuning models, there is a tool for deploying models to production, and there is a community forum for developers to share ideas and collaborate. Generative AI App Builder lets you create GenAI apps without having to write any code. GenaA-IApp Builder has a drag-and-drop interface that makes it easy to design and build apps. It has a visual editor that makes it easy to create and edit app content, it has a built-in search engine that allows users to search for information within the app, and it has a conversational AI engine that helps users to interact with the app using natural language. You can create your own digital assistants, custom search engines, knowledge bases, training applications, and much more. PaLM API lets you test and experiment with Google's large language models and GenAI tools. To make prototyping quick and more accessible, developers can integrate PaLM API with the maker suite and use it to access the API using a graphical user interface. The suite includes a number of different tools, such as a model training tool, a model deployment tool, and a model monitoring tool. The model training tool helps developers train ML models on their data using different algorithms. The model deployment tool helps developers deploy ML models to production with a number of different deployment options.

Benefits & Limitations

Generative AI is predicted by leading analysts' agencies to be the biggest transformative technology in the next few years. It brings many benefits which were unimaginable a few years ago. The ability of language models to interpret the query and come up with natural-sounding answers from a vast knowledge store has wider implications. We will discuss some of the broad benefits & limitations of Generative AI.

Benefits

- **Productivity and efficiency**: Reducing the need for human intervention and freeing up resources for other tasks, especially in scenarios such as contact centers and internal service desks. This can lead to significant time and cost savings for businesses as high as 70%. In addition, Generative AI can automate many tasks, such as transition, content generation, self-service, agent assistance, and many others, reducing overall manual efforts and turnaround time (TAT), leading to Operational Cost and Time Savings.
- **Personalization**: Personalize customer experiences, tailoring content and interactions to individual preferences and needs. Higher levels of engagement and customer satisfaction, as well as increased sales and loyalty. Generative AI can be used to personalize healthcare solutions by analyzing patient data and generating tailored treatment plans or recommendations. This can enhance patient experiences, improve outcomes, and drive patient satisfaction.
- **Innovation and development**: Enable new forms of creativity and innovation, providing new opportunities for products and services and driving growth and competitive advantage.
- **Enhanced Customer Experience**: The use of GenAI technologies to resolve customer grievances and potentially predict future issues can lead to better customer sentiment and improved retention.
- **Data-driven Insights & Decision Making**: Generative AI can

analyze large documents (such as research papers) and extract useful details, which can be used for decision-making. This can lead to efficient decision-making without impacting run costs.

- **Risk Mitigation**: Generative AI can aid in identifying and mitigating potential risks, such as fraud detection, product safety concerns, or supply chain disruptions, quickly. Fast analysis and alerting can lead to significant improvements in response times for unforeseen events.

Limitations

- **Data Privacy:** The internet data may contain personal information, if not masked, can remain in the models' response. There is still a long way to go till all the personal information is filtered. There are other aspects, like your business's private website, your browsing history, and chat history, that may also be used for training the generative AI model. The interesting aspect is that once trained, this information is difficult to erase or forgotten.
- **Ethical or Responsible Use of AI:** Lack of explain ability, use of inappropriate or unsafe language, biases in responses, and wrong responses with high confidence are areas of concern for many businesses.
- **Data Bias:** Generative AI models learn from existing data, which may contain biases or reflect existing disparities in healthcare. This can inadvertently perpetuate biases in the generated outputs, requiring careful monitoring and mitigation.
- **Copyright violations:** Some of the models are trained on large internet data, including codes, and make use of that data or code to generate responses that could be exactly the same as original data. This potentially infringes original copyright.
- **Wrong answers, hallucination** – generation of highly plausible but incorrect responses.

Conclusion

At a high level, the traditional classical supervised and unsupervised learning process takes training code and label data to build a model. Depending on the use case or problem, the model can give you a prediction; it can classify something or cluster something. We use this example to show you how much more robust the GenAI process is. The GenAI process can take training code, label data, and unlabelled data of all data types and build a foundation model. The foundation model can then generate new content, for example, text, code, images, audio, video, etc. We've come a long way from traditional programming to neural networks to generative models. In traditional programming, we used to have to hard code the rules for distinguishing a cat, the type, animal, legs, four, ears, two, fur, yes, likes, yarn and catnip. In the wave of neural networks, we could give the network pictures of cats and dogs and ask, is this a cat? And it would predict a cat. In the generative wave, we as users can generate our own content, whether it be text, images, audio, video, etc. For example, models like PaLM or pathways language model, or LaMDA language model for dialogue applications ingest very, very large data from multiple sources across the Internet. And build foundational language models we can use simply by asking a question, whether typing it into a prompt or verbally talking into the prompt itself.

Figure 2.11: *Concluding*

When you ask it, what's a cat? It can give you everything it has learned about a cat. Now we come to our formal definition, what is generative AI? GenAI is a type of artificial intelligence that creates new content based on what it has learned from existing content. The process of learning from existing content is called training and results in the creation of a statistical model. When given a prompt, GenAI uses the model to predict what an expected response might be, and this generates new content. Essentially, it learns the underlying structure of the data and can then generate new samples that are similar to the data it was trained on. As previously mentioned, a generative language model can take what it is learned from the examples.

DISCOVER YOUR WRITING POTENTIAL WITH ARCCHIE

We all possess unique talents for articulating various subjects, and you're among those gifted individuals. Whether you're a budding writer or a seasoned author, ARCCHIE PUBLICATIONS offers an ideal platform for your creative endeavors. If you aspire to become an author with ARCCHIE, we invite you to explore authors.arcchieonline.com and submit your application today. Our team is dedicated to assisting you in embarking on your authorship journey. Alternatively, scan QR code and connect with us.

Chapter 3

An introduction to Prompt Engineering

Humans communicate with each other through speaking and writing in multiple languages. Each language has sentences to set the tone, deliver the message, or ask questions. Similarly, when communicating with a system, one should use binary language that computers can understand. Developers write code in specific languages and use tools like interpreters or compilers to present the code to the system in its language. Regarding artificial intelligence (AI) and natural language processing (NLP), prompts are used to establish communication, such as how humans interact. Prompt Engineering is the specific process used for this.

The following topics will be covered in this chapter:

- Understanding Prompts
- Foundation and Importance of Prompt Engineering
- Prompt Engineering – challenges and limitations
- Prompt Engineering – Best practices

The aim of this chapter is to understand Prompt and Prompt Engineering. By end of this chapter readers will be able to clarify the purpose and functionality of Prompt Engineering.

Understanding Prompts

Understanding prompts is a crucial aspect that underpins the entire process of generating human-like text with language models. A prompt can be defined as a specific set of instructions or inputs provided to a language model to generate a desired output. These prompts can vary widely in complexity, from simple questions or statements to more elaborate scenarios or contexts.

The key to effectively using prompts lies in understanding how they influence the output of a language model. By carefully crafting prompts, users can guide the model in generating text that aligns with their intentions. This process is known as prompt engineering and is a fundamental technique used in various natural language processing (NLP) tasks, including text generation, summarization, and question-answering.

The complexity of prompt engineering is evident in the trade-off between specificity and flexibility. A highly specific prompt may yield more precise outputs but could limit the model's ability to generate diverse or creative responses. Conversely, a more flexible prompt can allow for a wider range of outputs but may result in less relevant or coherent text.

Prompt engineers employ practical strategies like prompt tuning and prompt design patterns to address the challenges of prompt engineering. Prompt tuning involves adjusting the wording or structure of a prompt to elicit the desired response from the model, while prompt design patterns are predefined templates or formats that work well with a particular model or task. These strategies can help guide the model's output and standardize the use of prompts.

Prompt design patterns, conversely, are predefined templates or formats designed to work well with a particular model or task. These patterns can standardize prompts and make it easier to generate high-quality text. Examples of prompt design patterns include question-answering prompts, completion prompts, and conditional prompts.

Another critical aspect of understanding prompts is considering the biases and limitations of the underlying language model. Like any AI system, language models can exhibit biases based on the data they were trained on. Prompt engineers must be aware of these biases and take steps to mitigate them, such as carefully selecting training data or using debiasing techniques.

Role of Prompts in Natural Language Processing (NLP)

Prompts play a crucial role in Natural Language Processing (NLP), particularly in the context of prompt engineering. Prompt engineering refers to designing and constructing prompts used in language models to elicit specific responses or behaviors. Prompts act as input instructions that guide the model in generating desired outputs. They can significantly impact the performance and behavior of NLP models, influencing aspects such as language generation, question-answering, and text summarization.

One key aspect of prompt engineering is the design of prompts to achieve specific tasks or goals. For example, in question-answering tasks, a well-designed prompt should provide enough context and structure to guide the model in generating accurate and relevant answers. This can involve using keywords or phrasing likely to elicit the desired information from the model. For instance, a prompt for a question-answering task about the capital of a country might include the country's name followed by a question mark, prompting the model to generate the capital city as the answer.

Another example of the role of prompts in NLP is in text summarization tasks. In this context, prompts can guide the model to generate concise summaries of longer texts. A well-designed prompt for text summarization should clearly indicate the desired output length and the key points to include in the summary. For instance, a prompt for summarizing a news article might consist of a brief description of the article's main topic followed by a request for a summary of a specific length.

Overall, prompts in NLP provide guidance and structure to language models, helping them generate more accurate and relevant outputs for specific tasks. By carefully designing prompts, researchers and developers can improve the performance and usability of NLP models across a wide range of applications.

Significance of well-designed prompt

The significance of a well-designed prompt cannot be overstated, especially in industries where efficiency, accuracy, and user experience are paramount. In this context, a prompt refers to a message or signal that prompts an action or response from a user or system. Whether in technology, customer service, or user interface design, a well-crafted prompt can enhance productivity, streamline processes, and improve overall outcomes.

In the technology industry, well-designed prompts are crucial for guiding users through software applications and ensuring they understand what action to take next. For example, consider a software program that guides users through steps to complete a task, such as filling out a form or setting up a new account. Clear and concise prompts at each step help users navigate the process smoothly and reduce the likelihood of errors or confusion. With well-designed prompts, users may be able to understand what is required of them, leading to frustration and potentially abandoned tasks.

In customer service, well-designed prompts can improve the

efficiency of interactions between customers and service representatives. For instance, consider a call center where agents use prompts to guide customer conversations. Companies can ensure consistent and effective communication by providing agents with prompts that suggest appropriate responses based on the customer's query or issue. This improves the customer experience and helps agents resolve issues more quickly and accurately.

In addition to improving efficiency and user experience, well-designed prompts can enhance security in industries where data protection is critical. For example, in the banking and finance industry, prompts are often used to verify users' identities before granting access to sensitive information. By designing prompts that require users to provide specific, pre-defined information (such as a PIN or password), companies can reduce the risk of unauthorized access and protect sensitive data.

Types of Prompts

A prompt in NLP is a piece of text or a query that guides a model in generating a desired output. It provides context and constraints for the model, helping it produce relevant and coherent responses. Prompts can vary in complexity and structure, depending on the task and the model used.

One common type is the completion prompt, where the model is asked to complete a given sentence or phrase. For example, a completion prompt for a language model could be "The quick brown fox jumps over the..." The model is then expected to generate the rest of the sentence based on its language understanding.

Another type of prompt is the question prompt, where the model is asked a question and is expected to provide an answer. Question prompts are commonly used in question-answering systems, where the model is trained to answer questions based on a given context. For example, a question prompt could be "Who is the president of the United States?" The model would then generate an answer such as "Joe Biden."

In addition to completion and question prompts, there are classification prompts, where the model is asked to classify a given piece of text into a predefined category. Classification prompts are often used in sentiment analysis and text classification tasks. For example, a classification prompt could be "Is this review positive or negative?" The model would then classify the review based on its sentiment.

Prompts can also be used in dialogue systems to generate responses in a conversation. In this case, the prompt would be the previous utterances in the conversation, and the model would create a response based on the context provided by the prompt. Dialogue prompts are often used in chatbots and virtual assistants to simulate natural conversations with users.

In this section, we will explore types of Prompts in detail:

Text-based prompts

Text-based prompts are instructions or questions that require a text-based response. These prompts are commonly used in various contexts, including education, assessments, surveys, and customer support. They require individuals to write a response rather than selecting from predefined options. Text-based prompts can vary in complexity, from simple questions that require short answers to more detailed prompts that require longer, structured responses.

Example of a Text-Based Prompt:

Consider a few examples for Text-based prompts; the result may vary.

Prompt: *Describe a memorable experience from your childhood and explain why it was meaningful to you.*

Explanation: This prompt asks the respondent to recall a specific event from their childhood and explain why it was significant to them. The response should include details about the experience and reflect on its impact on their life. This type of prompt not only encourages personal reflection and storytelling but also creates a unique and meaningful connection between the respondent and the prompt, fostering a sense of engagement and connection that is unique to text-based prompts.

Text-based prompts are valuable because they can elicit detailed and nuanced responses that provide insight into a person's thoughts, feelings, and experiences. Unlike multiple-choice questions, which limit responses to predefined options, text-based prompts liberate individuals to express themselves freely and in their own words, fostering a sense of creativity and depth in their responses.

In educational settings, text-based prompts are often used in writing assignments to assess students' ability to communicate effectively, organize their thoughts, and provide coherent arguments. For example, a prompt might ask students to write an essay analyzing a piece of literature or write a personal narrative about a significant event.

In assessments and surveys, text-based prompts can be used to gather qualitative data that provides deeper insights than quantitative data alone. For instance, in a customer feedback survey, a prompt might ask customers to describe their experience with a product or service in their own words, providing a wealth of valuable feedback that can lead to significant improvements. This unique ability of text-based prompts to gather qualitative data offers a deeper understanding of the respondent's perspective, enhancing the value of the data collected.

Text-based prompts can also be used in interviews and job applications to assess candidates' communication skills and critical thinking abilities. For example, a job application might include a prompt asking candidates to describe a challenging situation they faced at work and how they resolved it. This would allow employers to evaluate their problem-solving skills and ability to reflect on their experiences.

Contextual prompts

Contextual prompts are a feature of language models like ChatGPT (considerably any Language Model) that aim to provide more relevant and helpful responses by considering the context of the conversation. These prompts can help guide the conversation in a specific direction, clarify ambiguity, or provide additional information based on what has already been discussed.

For example, let's say you're asking about the best restaurants in a city. A contextual prompt might ask if you're looking for a specific type of cuisine or price range to narrow down the recommendations. This helps tailor the response to better match your preferences and needs.

Contextual prompts are not just reactive; they are proactive. They analyze the preceding conversation or information provided to determine the most relevant follow-up questions or suggestions. This intelligent use of natural language processing techniques helps them understand the context and intent behind your queries.

Contextual prompts are not just about maintaining the flow of a conversation; they are about ensuring that your needs are met efficiently. In a chatbot or virtual assistant setting, they can be your best friend, helping to prevent misunderstandings by seeking clarification when necessary.

For instance, if you ask a question about a topic with multiple interpretations, a contextual prompt might ask for more details to ensure that the answer provided is accurate and relevant to your query.

Overall, contextual prompts enhance the user experience by making interactions more personalized and tailored to individual preferences. They help ensure you get the information you need clearly and concisely, leading to more effective communication and problem-solving.

Task specific prompts

Task-specific prompts are questions or instructions designed to guide you through a specific task or activity. They are meant to help you focus on the task at hand and provide you with the necessary information to complete it effectively. They are often used in educational settings, such as classrooms or online courses, to help students understand what is expected of them and how to approach a particular assignment.

Let's take an example to explain task-specific prompts in more detail. Imagine you are a student working on a research paper about climate change.

Your teacher provides you with the following task-specific prompt:

"Research and write a paper on the impact of climate change on coastal communities. Your paper should include information about the causes of climate change, its effects on sea levels and weather patterns, and how it affects coastal communities worldwide. Use at least three reputable sources to support your arguments and cite them properly in your paper."

In this example, the task-specific prompt outlines the specific requirements and expectations for the research paper. It specifies the topic (impact of climate change on coastal communities), the key areas to focus on (causes, effects, and implications on communities), and the number of sources to use (at least three). It also guides how to structure the paper (including proper citation of sources).

Task-specific prompts are helpful because they provide clear guidance and direction, which can help you stay focused and organized while working on a task. They also help ensure that you meet the task's requirements and produce high-quality work.

When responding to task-specific prompts, it's essential to read them carefully and make sure you understand what is being asked of you. If you have any questions or need clarification, please ask for help. Additionally, follow the instructions in the prompt and use the guidance provided to structure your work effectively.

Foundation and Importance of Prompt Engineering

Prompt engineering is crucial to designing effective human-computer interactions, particularly in natural language processing (NLP) and artificial intelligence (AI) systems. At its core, prompt engineering focuses on crafting prompts that efficiently and accurately elicit desired responses from users or systems. This discipline draws from various fields, including linguistics, psychology, and human-computer interaction, to create clear, concise, and contextually appropriate prompts.

The main goal is to make interactions with computers more natural and helpful. By designing prompts well, we can ensure that the computer gives accurate and relevant responses, making it easier for people to use and get what they need from technology.

Let us explore it:

Linguistic considerations of creating effective prompts

Linguistic considerations play a crucial role in creating effective prompts for human-computer interaction. These considerations involve various aspects of language use, such as clarity, conciseness, and cultural sensitivity, all contributing to the overall user experience.

One key aspect of linguistic considerations is clarity. Prompts should be clear and easy to understand, avoiding ambiguity and confusion. This means using simple language that is accessible to the target audience. Avoiding jargon and technical terms that may be unfamiliar to users can also enhance clarity.

When considering conciseness in prompt design, it's important to put yourself in the user's shoes. Long-winded prompts can be overwhelming and lead to frustration. By keeping prompts concise, you're making your job easier and helping users quickly understand what is expected of them, fostering a smoother interaction with the system.

Consistency is essential for maintaining coherence in prompt design. Prompts should use consistent language and terminology to avoid confusion. For example, if a system uses a specific term to refer to a particular action, it should use that term consistently throughout the interaction. Inconsistencies in language use can confuse users and detract from the overall user experience.

Context sensitivity is also essential in prompt design. Prompts should be sensitive to the interaction context, providing relevant information based on the user's current situation or needs. For example, a prompt for a weather forecasting system should consider the user's location and provide relevant weather information for that location.

As professionals involved in prompt design, we have a responsibility to ensure our prompts are culturally sensitive. This means avoiding language or references that may be offensive or inappropriate in certain cultural contexts. By understanding the cultural norms and sensitivities of our diverse user base, we can adapt our prompts accordingly, fostering a more inclusive and respectful user experience.

Prompt Designing – an overview to cognitive factors

When designing prompts, it is crucial to consider cognitive factors influencing how users perceive, process, and respond to them. Cognitive factors play a significant role in determining the effectiveness of prompts in eliciting the desired responses from users.

In this section, we will explore some key cognitive factors and how they can be applied in prompt design, along with examples:

Cognitive Load

Cognitive load refers to the mental effort required to process information. Prompts should be designed to minimize cognitive load, especially for complex tasks or when users are under time pressure.

`Example`: In a chatbot interface, instead of asking a user to input a long and complex command, the prompt can use a series of more straightforward, more digestible questions to gather the necessary information step by step.

Information Processing

Users process information differently based on their cognitive abilities and prior knowledge. Prompts should be designed to accommodate these differences and provide information in a format that is easy to understand and process.

`Example`: When designing prompts for a language learning app, the prompts should be tailored to the user's proficiency level, providing more straightforward prompts for beginners and more complex prompts for advanced users.

Feedback

Prompt design should include feedback mechanisms that inform users about the status of their interaction and guide them on what to do next. Timely and informative feedback can help users stay engaged and confident in their interactions with the system.

`Example`: In a voice assistant, after a user gives a command, the assistant should provide verbal feedback confirming the command was understood and proceed with the requested action.

Error Handling

Users are prone to making errors, especially when performing complex tasks or when unfamiliar with the system. Prompt design should include clear and helpful error messages that guide users in correcting their mistakes.

`Example`: If a user enters an invalid date format when scheduling an appointment, the system should display a message explaining the correct format and prompt the user to try again.

Learning Curve

Prompt design should consider the user's learning curve and provide prompts appropriate for their level of familiarity with the system. Over time, prompts can be adjusted to match the user's increasing proficiency.

`Example`: In a video game, prompts can start with basic controls and gradually introduce more advanced commands as the player progresses through the game.

User Preferences

Prompt design should consider individual user preferences and adapt to their needs and preferences over time. Personalized prompts can enhance user engagement and satisfaction.

`Example`: A virtual assistant can learn from user interactions and tailor prompts based on the user's preferences, such as preferred language or communication style.

Consideration in prompt engineering

Considerations in prompt engineering cover various factors designers must consider to create effective, user-friendly prompts.

Let's delve into these considerations in detail with examples:

- **Clarity and Simplicity**: Instead of asking, "Please provide your location coordinates," a clearer prompt would be, "Where are you located?"
- **Context Awareness**: A chatbot for a weather app might ask, "Do you want to know the current weather in your location?" If the user had previously provided their location, the prompt could be even more specific: "Would you like to know the current weather in New York City?"
- **User Familiarity**: A prompt for a technical support chatbot might use jargon familiar to the user, such as "Have you tried rebooting your device?" instead of using technical terms like "power cycle."
- **Feedback and Confirmation**: After a user selects a seat for booking a flight, the prompt could confirm the selection with a message like, "You've selected seat 12A. Is that correct?"
- **Accessibility**: A voice-based virtual assistant should provide alternative text-based prompts for users who are deaf or hard of hearing.

Importance of Prompt Engineering

Prompt Engineering is important because good prompts make interactions with AI systems easier and more effective, leading to better results and a smoother user experience; good prompts are necessary for them to be more helpful and helpful. So, by designing good prompts, we can make AI systems more useful and user-friendly.

- **Enhanced User Experience**: Well-crafted prompts can significantly improve the user experience by making interactions with AI systems more natural, intuitive, and engaging.
- **Increased Efficiency**: Effective prompts can streamline interactions, helping users achieve their goals more efficiently and reducing the time and effort required to complete tasks.
- **Improved Accuracy**: Clear and specific prompts can lead to more accurate responses from AI systems, minimizing errors and misunderstandings.
- **Context Sensitivity**: Prompt engineering enables prompts to be contextually sensitive, adapting to the user's current task or situation to provide relevant and helpful information.
- **User Engagement**: Thoughtfully designed prompts can enhance user engagement by encouraging users to interact more with AI systems, leading to more meaningful interactions and better data collection.
- **Data Quality**: Prompt engineering ensures data collection quality for training AI models. Well-designed prompts can help collect diverse and relevant data, leading to more robust and accurate models.
- **Ethical Considerations**: Prompt engineering also encompasses ethical considerations, such as ensuring that prompts are unbiased, respectful, and do not infringe on user privacy

Prompt Engineering – challenges and limitations

While prompt engineering can significantly enhance the performance and usability of language models, it also comes with several challenges and limitations.

One key challenge of prompt engineering is the need for domain expertise. Crafting effective prompts often requires a deep understanding of the underlying concepts and nuances of the target domain. With this expertise, it can be easier to formulate prompts that elicit accurate and relevant responses from the language model.

Another formidable challenge is the inherent complexity of language itself. Natural language is inherently ambiguous and context-dependent, posing a significant hurdle in designing prompts that consistently produce the desired outputs. Moreover, the effectiveness of a prompt can vary depending on the specific language model being used, further adding to the intricacy of prompt engineering.

Furthermore, there exists a delicate balance between the specificity and generality of prompts. Highly specific prompts may yield accurate responses for a narrow range of inputs but fail to generalize well to unseen data. Conversely, overly general prompts may produce more diverse outputs but at the cost of accuracy and relevance, underscoring the importance of this trade-off in prompt engineering.

Additionally, prompt interpretability is a significant limitation. While designing prompts that produce reliable outputs is possible, understanding why a particular prompt elicits a specific response can be challenging. This lack of interpretability can hinder the trustworthiness and usability of language models in real-world applications.

Moreover, the effectiveness of prompts can be influenced by various factors, including the quality and quantity of training data, the architecture of the language model, and the specific task at hand. As a result, designing effective prompts often requires extensive experimentation and fine-tuning, which can be time-consuming and resource-intensive.

Potential pitfalls in prompt design

Effective, prompt design is a cornerstone in various fields, such as natural language processing, education, and research. A meticulously crafted prompt has the power to elicit desired responses and enhance the performance of models. However, numerous pitfalls can impede its effectiveness. Grasping these pitfalls is paramount for crafting prompts that yield the desired outcomes.

One common pitfall in prompt design is ambiguity. Ambiguous prompts can lead to inconsistent or unexpected responses from models. For example, a prompt like "Write a story about a man and a woman" is ambiguous because it does not specify the relationship between the characters or the setting. This ambiguity can result in a wide range of responses, making controlling the model's output challenging.

Another pitfall is bias. Biased prompts can lead to biased responses, perpetuating stereotypes or discrimination. For example, a prompt that assumes specific gender roles or cultural norms can influence the content of the generated text, potentially reinforcing societal biases. To avoid bias, prompts should be carefully crafted to be inclusive and avoid assumptions about gender, race, or other sensitive topics.

Complexity is another potential pitfall. Complex prompts can confuse models and lead to incorrect or nonsensical responses. For example, a prompt that contains multiple clauses or conditional statements may be challenging for a model to understand, resulting in a communication breakdown. Prompts should be clear, concise, and straightforward to avoid this pitfall.

Lack of specificity is also a common pitfall in prompt design. A need to be more specific or general prompt can result in generic or uninformative responses. For example, a prompt like "Describe a house" does not provide enough detail for the model to generate a meaningful response. To avoid this pitfall, prompts should be specific and provide enough context for the model to develop a relevant and detailed response.

Finally, context collapse can be a significant pitfall in prompt design. Context collapse occurs when a prompt fail to provide enough context for the model to generate an appropriate response. For example, a prompt that asks a model to continue a story without giving any information about the characters or setting can result in a disconnected reaction from the original story. To avoid context collapse, prompts should provide sufficient context for the model to understand the task and generate a relevant response.

Addressing Bias and fairness in prompts

Addressing bias and fairness in prompts is critical to developing AI models that can interact with users somewhat and unbiasedly. Prompts are foundational in shaping the responses generated by AI models, and they can inadvertently introduce bias if not carefully constructed. Bias in prompts can arise from various sources, including the language used, the examples provided, and the cultural references embedded within them. Addressing bias in prompts requires a multi-faceted approach that considers linguistic, artistic, and ethical dimensions.

One key aspect of addressing bias in prompts is carefully choosing the language used. Language can unintentionally convey bias through stereotypes, assumptions, or exclusionary terms. Prompts should be crafted with sensitivity to diverse perspectives and experiences to mitigate this. Avoiding loaded language and ensuring that prompts are inclusive can help reduce the risk of bias.

Another important consideration is the examples provided in the prompts. Examples should be diverse and representative of different demographics and cultural backgrounds. This helps avoid reinforcing stereotypes and ensures that the AI model is exposed to various perspectives. Additionally, examples should be carefully vetted to ensure they do not inadvertently promote biased or discriminatory views.

Cultural references are another potential source of bias in prompts. References to specific cultural norms, holidays, or traditions may not be universally understood or appreciated. When including cultural references in prompts, it is essential to provide context and explanations to ensure all users can understand the prompt and its implications.

Addressing bias in prompts involves ethical considerations in addition to linguistic and cultural considerations. AI models are increasingly being used to make decisions that impact people's lives, such as hiring, lending, and criminal justice. Prompts in these contexts must be fair and unbiased to avoid perpetuating or exacerbating existing inequalities.

One approach to addressing bias in prompts is to use a diverse set of human annotators to review and provide feedback on the prompts. Annotators can help identify potential sources of bias and suggest alternative wording or examples that are more inclusive and representative. Additionally, machine learning techniques can detect and mitigate prompts' bias. For example, algorithms can be trained to identify biased language or examples and suggest alternative options.

Prompt Engineering: Best Practices

Prompt engineering is crucial in designing effective and efficient natural language processing (NLP) systems, particularly those based on large language models (LLMs) like GPT-3. It involves crafting prompts, which are the inputs provided to these models, in such a way that they elicit the desired responses. The goal is to guide the model to produce outputs that meet specific criteria, such as relevance, accuracy, coherence, and tone. This section will discuss the best practices for prompt engineering, covering various aspects such as prompt formulation, context utilization, and evaluation.

- **Understand the Problem**: Before designing prompts, you must clearly understand the problem you are trying to solve. Define the goals of the NLP system and the desired outcomes.
- **Define the Task**: Clearly define the task that the model needs to perform. Is it text completion, question-answering, summarization, or something else? The prompt should align with the task requirements.
- **Craft Clear and Concise Prompts**: Prompts should be formulated in a way that is easy for the model to understand. Use simple language and avoid ambiguity. Clearly state what you expect the model to do.
- **Provide Context**: Context is crucial for helping the model generate relevant responses. Provide enough context in the prompt to give the model the necessary information to generate a meaningful output.
- **Use Natural Language**: When designing prompts, use natural language miming how humans interact. This helps the model understand the task better and produce more human-like responses.
- **Use Examples**: Providing examples of the desired output can help the model generate the correct responses. Include diverse examples to cover a wide range of possible outputs.
- **Avoid Biases**: Be mindful of biases in the language and examples used in prompts. Biased prompts can lead to biased outputs from the model.
- **Iterate and Experiment**: Prompt engineering is an iterative process. Experiment with different prompts and evaluate the outputs to see what works best. Continuously refine your prompts based on feedback.
- **Consider Fine-tuning**: Fine-tuning the model on specific prompts and examples related to your task can improve its performance. Fine-tuning allows the model to learn from the provided examples and adapt to the task's specific requirements.
- **Evaluate Outputs**: Regularly evaluate the outputs generated by the model to ensure they meet the desired criteria. Human evaluators are used to assess the quality of the responses.

- **Monitor Performance**: Monitor the model's performance over time and adjust the prompts as needed. As the model learns and adapts, the effectiveness of the prompts may change.

Conclusion

The chapter on Prompt Engineering has provided a comprehensive exploration of the field, shedding light on its historical background, definition, and significance. We have delved into the purpose and objectives of prompt engineering, emphasizing its role in Natural Language Processing (NLP) and Artificial Intelligence (AI) applications.

Throughout this chapter, we have examined the concept of prompts, their role in facilitating communication like human interactions, and the importance of well-designed prompts in guiding AI models and influencing their outputs. We have explored real-world examples across different industries to illustrate the practical applications of prompt engineering, including its relevance in the supply chain industry.

Additionally, we have touched upon the technical aspects of prompt engineering, discussing the programming languages commonly used for writing prompt engineering code, the phases involved in building prompts, and the steps of the prompt engineering process. Code examples in Python have been provided to enhance understanding and practical implementation.

Moreover, we have explored the visualization of prompt engineering through architectural diagrams, highlighting its components and interactions. The chapter has also addressed the significance of prompt engineering in promoting accessibility, particularly for visually impaired individuals, exemplified by the development of a cognitive engine-powered visualizer.

This chapter is a comprehensive introduction to prompt engineering, laying the foundation for further exploration and understanding in this dynamic and evolving field. We hope readers have gained valuable insights into the principles, techniques, and applications of prompt engineering, empowering them to leverage its potential in their own endeavors.

In the next chapter, you will read various aspects related to language models, natural language processing (NLP), and conversational AI, followed by a deep dive into generative AI concepts, fine-tuning language models, and Building Chatbots.

JOIN US ON THE

ARCCHIE PUBLICATIONS

DISCORD SERVER

Connect with fellow readers, authors, and enthusiasts to discuss all things related to our publications and the exciting world of AI, programming, and learning. Share your insights, ask questions, and engage in vibrant discussions to expand your knowledge and inspire creativity. Take advantage of this opportunity to be part of a dynamic community dedicated to exploring the frontiers of technology and innovation. Join our Discord Server today and be part of the ARCCHIE PUBLICATIONS community!

https://discord.gg/z26SenmpEt

Chapter 4
Need of AI Models

AI models are algorithms or mathematical representations that enable artificial intelligence systems to perform specific tasks or make predictions. Today, we use AI models for several analytical and decision-making tasks. AI models rely on computer vision, natural language processing, and Machine Learning to recognize different patterns.

AI models also use decision-making algorithms to learn from their training, collect and review data points, and ultimately apply their learning to achieve their predefined goals.

The following topics will be covered in this chapter:
- AI Models at Problem Solving
- Types of Models
- Selecting a Model
- Importance of AI Models in Business World
- Benefits of AI Models
- Future of AI Modeling
- AI/ML Model scoring
- Real-time or Batch scoring
- Automatic Deployment and Integration with your existing Production systems

AI Models at Problem Solving

AI models are very good at solving complex problems with a large amount of data. As a result, they can accurately solve complex problems with a very high degree of accuracy. These models are trained on large amounts of data and learn patterns, correlations, and rules from the data to make intelligent decisions. Here are some common types of AI models:

- **Linear Regression**: A linear regression model is used for predicting a continuous target variable based on input features. It establishes a linear relationship between the input variables and the output variable.

- **Logistic Regression**: Logistic regression is employed for binary classification problems, where the model predicts the probability of an instance belonging to a particular class.

- **Decision Trees**: Decision tree models use a tree-like structure to make decisions by splitting the data based on feature values. They are easy to interpret and can handle both classification and regression tasks.

- **Random Forests**: Random forests combine multiple decision trees to make predictions. They use ensemble learning, aggregating predictions from individual trees to improve accuracy and reduce overfitting.

- **Support Vector Machines (SVM)**: SVM models are used for classification tasks and find a hyperplane that maximally separates different classes in the data. They can handle both linear and non-linear classification problems.

- **Naive Bayes**: Naive Bayes models are probabilistic classifiers that use Bayes' theorem to calculate the probability of an instance belonging to a certain class. They assume independence between features, hence the "naive" assumption.

- **Neural Networks**: Neural networks are a collection of interconnected nodes (neurons) arranged in layers. They can learn complex patterns from data and are widely used for tasks like image recognition, natural language processing, and speech recognition.

- **Convolutional Neural Networks (CNN)**: CNNs are specialized neural networks designed for processing grid-like data, such as images. They use convolutional layers to extract relevant features and achieve state-of-the-art performance in image classification, object detection, and image generation tasks.

- **Recurrent Neural Networks (RNN)**: RNNs are designed to handle sequential data, such as text or time series. They have recurrent connections that allow information to persist over time, making them suitable for tasks like language modelling, speech recognition, and machine translation.

- **Transformer Models**: Transformer models, such as the popular GPT (Generative Pre-Trained Transformer), utilize self-attention mechanisms to capture long-range dependencies in sequential data. They excel in natural language processing tasks like language translation, text generation, and sentiment analysis.

These are just a few examples of AI models, and there are many more variants and architectures available. The choice of model depends on the specific task, the nature of the data, and the desired outcome.

Types of Models

AI models can help businesses to become more efficient, competitive, and profitable, by allowing them to make better decisions based on data analysis. In the future, AI models will likely become even more important in business, as more and more companies adopt them to gain a competitive advantage. There are various types of AI models used in different applications. Here are some common types:

Machine Learning Models

Machine learning models are trained on data to make predictions or take actions without being explicitly programmed. They can be categorized into subtypes such as:

- Supervised Learning: Models learn from labeled data to make predictions or classify new instances.
- Unsupervised Learning: Models find patterns and relationships in unlabeled data without specific guidance.
- Reinforcement Learning: Models learn to make decisions and take actions based on feedback from their environment.

Tip: A Machine Learning algorithm uses complex mathematical and statistical techniques like logistic regression for pattern recognition. However, Machine Learning is much more than these highly technical operations. Although it is driven by a scientific approach, it is also a very creative field. Machine Learning algorithms are capable of surpassing humans in many ways. By implementing Machine Learning within your app you will be able to increase its performance and improve functionalities in important ways while gaining efficiency.

Machine learning is already transforming our world miraculously. The method is used to construct different models capable of identifying and predicting cancer growths in medical scans, detecting fraudulent transactions, and even helping people learn languages. Algorithms that have been trained to perform specific tasks like sorting images, predicting housing prices, or making chess moves.

At a glance, here are some of the major benefits of a machine learning:

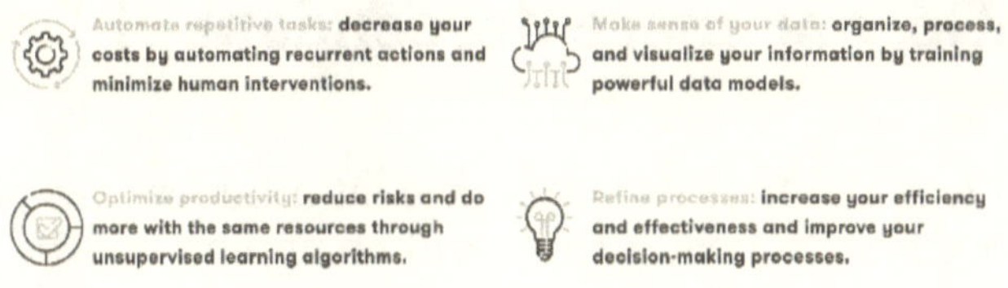

Figure 5.1: Benefits of Machine Learning

Deep Learning Models

Deep learning models are a subset of machine learning models that are based on artificial neural networks with multiple layers. They excel at processing complex data, such as images, speech, and text. Convolutional Neural Networks (CNNs) for image recognition and Recurrent Neural Networks (RNNs) for sequential data are popular types of deep learning models.

Machine learning refers to the general use of algorithms and data to create autonomous or semi-autonomous machines. Deep learning, meanwhile, is a subset of machine learning that layers algorithms into "neural networks" that somewhat resemble the human brain so that machines can perform increasingly complex tasks.

Deep Blue, the chess-playing computer

Before the development of machine learning, artificially intelligent machines or programs had to be programmed to respond to a limited set of inputs. Deep Blue, a chess-playing computer that beat a world chess champion in 1997, could "decide" its next move based on an extensive library of possible moves and outcomes. But the system was purely reactive. For Deep Blue to improve at playing chess, programmers had to go in and add more features and possibilities.

AlphaGo, one more descendant of Deep Blue

AlphaGo was the first program to beat a human Go player, as well as the first to beat a Go world champion in 2015. Go is a 3,000-year-old board game originating in China and known for its complex strategy. It's much more complicated than chess, with 10 to the power of 170 possible configurations on the board.

The creators of AlphaGo began by introducing the program to several games of Go to teach it the mechanics. Then it began playing against different versions of itself thousands of times, learning from its mistakes after each game. AlphaGo became so good that the best human players in the world are known to study its inventive moves.

The latest version of the AlphaGo algorithm, known as MuZero, can master games like Go, chess, and Atari without even needing to be told the rules.

Natural Language Processing Models

NLP models are designed to understand and generate human language. They enable tasks like language translation, sentiment analysis, text summarization, question answering, and Chabot. Transformers, such as the GPT (Generative Pre-trained Transformer) models, have achieved significant advancements in NLP. Natural Language Processing: Just as computers make sense of different types of data, it is possible to make sense of language. After all, language is just another form of data. However, for machines to understand language, computers first need to interpret it and transform it into something they can understand. NLP is the text classification process through which a computer processes what is being said, determines its context, gives sense to it, and responds based on the resulting meaning. In short, it is the way computers make sense of human language.

Computer Vision Models

Computer vision models process and analyse visual data, such as images and videos. They are used for tasks like object detection, image classification, facial recognition, and autonomous driving. Popular models include Convolutional Neural Networks (CNNs), such as the well-known architecture called ResNet.

Computer vision is a field of computer science that concerns itself with studying, researching, and attempting to develop methods that allow computers to see and understand visual information using logical thinking to solve real-world problems. On the surface, it would seem as if this problem were simple; after all, even children and animals are proficient at it. Computer vision solutions are used every day in a number of different ways. In fact, it is likely that you have come across some form of this technology in your daily life. Do you use Snapchat? Do you like to add filters to your pictures that allow you to put on dog ears or other funny faces? This is a good example of this technology. If you have a newer iPhone model, your phone likely has facial recognition features that help you unlock your phone and set up secure Apple payments. This is another example.

Recommendation Systems

These models provide personalized recommendations to users based on their preferences and behavior. Collaborative Filtering, Content-Based Filtering, and Hybrid approaches are commonly used in recommendation systems.

Generative Models

Generative models create new data samples similar to the training data they were exposed to. Variational Autoencoders (VAEs) and Generative Adversarial Networks (GANs) are widely used generative models in fields like image generation, text generation, and data synthesis.

Expert Systems

Expert systems are AI models that emulate human expertise and knowledge in specific domains. They use a set of rules and logic to provide advice or make decisions. Expert systems are often used in fields like medicine, finance, and engineering.

Robotics Models

Robotics models combine AI with physical robots to perform tasks autonomously or with human assistance. These models integrate perception, planning, and control algorithms to enable robots to interact with the environment and accomplish tasks.

These are just a few examples, and AI models continue to evolve and diversify as new research and applications emerge. Different types of AI models are utilized based on the specific problem, data availability, and desired outcomes.

Selecting a Model

Selecting the right model for a specific task can be a crucial decision, as it greatly influences the performance and efficiency of your AI system.

Here is a step-by-step guide to help you select the right model:

Understand Your Problem

Clearly define your problem and its objectives. Understand the type of data you have (e.g., text, images, time series) and the specific task you want to perform (e.g., classification, regression, generation).

Data Pre-processing

Prepare and pre-process your data. This may involve cleaning, normalization, data augmentation, or embedding (for text data).

Define Success Metrics

Determine the metrics that will be used to evaluate the performance of your model. Common metrics include accuracy, F1 score, mean squared error, and so on, depending on the problem.

Select an Architecture

Choose an appropriate deep learning architecture based on your problem. Some common architectures include:

- Convolutional Neural Networks (CNNs) for image data.
- Recurrent Neural Networks (RNNs) for sequential data like text or time series.
- Transformers for natural language processing tasks.
- Feedforward Neural Networks (FNNs) for tabular data and structured data.

Hyper parameter Tuning

Experiment with different hyper parameters such as the number of layers, neurons per layer, learning rate, batch size, and activation functions. Use techniques like grid search or random search to find the best combination.

Regularization

Apply regularization techniques like dropout, L1/L2 regularization, or batch normalization to prevent overfitting.

Data Splitting

Split your data into training, validation, and test sets. Cross-validation is also an option for smaller datasets.

Model Training

Train your model on the training data while monitoring the performance on the validation set. Be aware of potential issues like vanishing/exploding gradients and adjust your model accordingly.

Model Evaluation

Evaluate your model on the test set to get an unbiased estimate of its performance. Compare it against the success metrics you defined earlier.

Iterate and Refine

If your model doesn't perform well, iterate through the process. This may involve collecting more data, changing the architecture, or experimenting with different hyper parameters.

Consider Pre-Trained Models

In many cases, pre-trained models (e.g., pre-trained language models for NLP tasks) can save time and resources. Fine-tuning these models for your specific task is often more efficient than training from scratch.

Resource Constraints

Consider the resources available for deployment. Smaller models may be necessary if you have limited computational resources, such as in edge computing applications.

Ethical Considerations

Ensure that your model aligns with ethical and legal guidelines, particularly in cases involving sensitive data or decision-making.

Monitoring and Maintenance

Once your model is deployed, continuously monitor its performance, as well as any data drift or concept drift.

Documentation

Keep detailed records of the entire process, including data, preprocessing steps, model architecture, hyper parameters, and performance results.

Selecting the right deep learning model is often an iterative process that involves experimentation and fine-tuning. It's crucial to have a good understanding of your problem and adapt your approach as needed to achieve the best results.

Importance of AI Models in Business World

Artificial intelligence (AI) models have become increasingly important in the business world. Here are few examples how it impacts overall business:

Recommendation engines are one of the most popular applications of machine learning, as product recommendations are featured on most e-commerce websites. Using machine learning models, websites track your behavior to recognize patterns in your browsing history, previous purchases, and shopping cart activity. This data collection is used for pattern recognition to predict user preferences.

Companies like Spotify and Netflix use similar machine learning algorithms to recommend music or TV shows based on your previous listening and viewing history. Over time and with training, these algorithms aim to understand your preferences to accurately predict which artists or films you may enjoy.

AI can recognize images, language models can also support and manipulate speech signals into commands and text. Software applications coded with AI can convert recorded and live speech into text files. Voice-based technologies can be used in medical applications, such as helping doctors extract important medical terminology from a conversation with a patient. While this tool isn't advanced enough to make trustworthy clinical decisions, other speech recognition services provide patients with reminders to "*take their medication*".

AI has become integral part of our lives unknowingly due to several key needs:

Automation

AI models can automate repetitive tasks, enabling businesses to streamline operations, reduce costs, and improve efficiency. Tasks such as data entry, customer support, and inventory management can be automated using AI, freeing up human resources for more complex and strategic activities.

Data analysis

AI models have the ability to analyze large volumes of data quickly and extract valuable insights. Businesses can use AI algorithms to discover patterns, trends, and correlations in data, helping them make data-driven decisions and develop effective strategies. This can lead to improved performance, better customer targeting, and more accurate predictions.

Personalization and customer experience

AI models enable businesses to personalize their offerings and enhance the customer experience. By analyzing customer data, AI algorithms can generate personalized recommendations, tailored marketing campaigns, and customized product suggestions. This personalization can lead to higher customer satisfaction, increased engagement, and improved conversion rates.

Predictive analytics

AI models can perform predictive analytics by leveraging historical data to forecast future outcomes. This capability helps businesses anticipate demand, optimize inventory, manage supply chains, and mitigate risks. By making accurate predictions, businesses can optimize their operations and make proactive decisions to gain a competitive edge.

Natural language processing and Chabot

AI-powered natural language processing (NLP) models enable businesses to automate customer interactions through chatbots and virtual assistants. These models can understand and respond to customer queries, provide support, and offer personalized recommendations. NLP models enhance customer service, improve response times, and provide 24/7 availability, thereby increasing customer satisfaction.

Fraud detection and cybersecurity

AI models play a crucial role in detecting fraudulent activities and enhancing cybersecurity. Machine learning algorithms can analyze vast amounts of data in real-time, identify anomalies, and flag potential security threats or fraudulent transactions. This helps businesses protect sensitive information, prevent financial losses, and ensure data integrity.

Competitive advantage

In today's competitive business landscape, AI models can provide a significant advantage. Companies that effectively leverage AI technology can gain insights faster, respond to market changes more rapidly, and make data-driven decisions ahead of their competitors. AI can fuel innovation, improve operational efficiency, and help businesses stay ahead in their respective industries.

Benefits of AI Models

Overall, AI models offer numerous benefits to businesses, including automation, data analysis, personalization, predictive analytics, enhanced customer experiences, improved cybersecurity, and a competitive edge. As a result, organizations across various sectors are increasingly adopting AI technologies to drive growth, increase productivity, and deliver value to their customers.

how to choose an AI model? Going through first the reasons for model selection, how it works and then some considerations that we need to have.

When we think about model selection, we're deciding between different types of models as well as selection within a specific model type.

The first large decisions we have to make, is the problem supervised or unsupervised learning problem? If it's supervised, we have to think about regression versus classification. Sometimes you can do both, but there's usually a standard answer. With unsupervised learning, we have to decide between clustering, anomaly detection, and the various other types of machine learning algorithms that you can employ.

There are also many models within each of these sub groups. For example, within classification, their support vector machines, K nearest neighbors or KNNs. We have linear classifiers, neural network classification, random forest classifiers. The type of algorithm or method you will use really depends on the data and some of the considerations that we'll go through in the next slides. Throughout this course, we'll teach you when to pick these different models and when it's useful to just test all of them and see which one works best. Within a specific model type, there are additional considerations we need to have. The first is tuning hyper parameters. Hyper parameters consist of anything from the number of nodes in a neural network, the number of trees in a random forest classifier to deciding the penalty on the linear aggressor. We'll often use a train test validation split in order to optimize our hyper parameters and make them perform best, not only in our current data, but when deployed on all data.

Other types of model selection include selecting the loss function. We'll talk more about loss functions when we do neural networks in the next couple videos, but also regularization techniques with linear repressors. There are different types of penalties you can impose for predictions being wrong, and the type of penalty you choose can often make a model perform better or worse.

Some of the different considerations when doing model selection, it's not just accuracy, although that is a big part of it. Accuracy refers to quite simply how often our predictions are matching the actual answers. The reason accuracy alone is not the perfect metric is we can only judge accuracy on our current data set and have no sense on how it will perform when put in the real world unless we use trained test splits.

Another key metric is reliability. Reliability refers to how often a model will generate meaningful enough results. In some cases, you can have model A that is very good at generating results half of the time and very bad the other half of the time. As opposed to Model B who generates okay results, but is very consistent in doing so. The exact model you choose, again, depends on the use case.

Another big consideration is speed.

With infinite computing time and all the computers in the world, there may be a lot more powerful algorithms that we can employ.

But given practical considerations on speed and deployment time, oftentimes going down to simpler algorithms or reducing the number of nodes in a network is helpful to make sure the performance is equal.

Finally, an often-underrated component of model selection is explaining ability.

Lots of AI algorithms are described as black boxes, and in some cases, we'll have no choice but to use those. However, when performance is similar between a simple and a more complicated algorithm, experts almost always choose the simple algorithm because it's more easily explained, and they can infer some of the insights manually.

Future of AI modeling

As AI continues its rapid evolution, businesses need to keep up with its prevailing trends. From cutting-edge machine learning algorithms to advancements in natural language processing, these trends hold the potential to reshape industries and our daily lives.

Creative or Generative AI

This AI refers to the use of artificial intelligence techniques to generate original content such as images, text and music. In this process, AI models are trained to learn patterns and structures from existing data and create unique and original content from that learned knowledge. For example, generative AI can generate images, paintings or designs based on certain styles and criteria. Creative AI can generate music based on existing songs, and techniques to create original soundtracks.

AI for Personalization

The impact of artificial intelligence on technology is nothing short of a revolution. AI allows companies to better offer users a personalized experience catered to their individual needs. By analyzing user behavior and preferences, AI technology enables e-commerce platforms to recommend products that are most likely to appeal to specific users based on their search history and previous purchases.

This level of personalization not only enhances user experience but also boosts customer satisfaction and loyalty.

AI modeling provides organizations a means of efficient decision making. For an organization to maximize benefits from AI modeling, the model requires extensive AI training which will produce complete automation. Effective AI modeling has already assisted organizations across several fields. Predictions for The Future of AI With the constant advancements in technology, we can anticipate even greater breakthroughs in the future, and it will undoubtedly play an increasingly significant role in shaping the future.

How can we prepare ourselves for the future? It's simple. Spread awareness and continuously educate ourselves. AI may seem surreal for its incredible ability to automate tasks that are repetitive and free up time for humans. However, it is a helpful tool for us to focus on more complex and creative endeavors. For example, AI can help many people in different industries including doctors. It can help analyze medical images and potentially save a patient's life. AI is also expected to play a crucial role in the field of transportation. Self-driving cars like Teslas are becoming popular, and we can expect to see more highly advanced technology cars in the future. AI can also optimize logistics and supply chains, making them more efficient and cost-effective.

AI/ML/LLM Model Scoring

One of the main reasons why we build AI/Machine Learning models is for it to be used in production to support expert decision making. Whether your business is deciding what creatives your customers should be getting on emails or determining a product recommendation for a web page, AI/Models provide relevance/context to customers to drive your business. For healthcare applications, this could mean recommending a patient to consult a health advisor for preventive care, to avoid hospitalization. For retail, this could mean triggering inventory decisions ahead of brewing peak demand. For financial applications, this may indicate a trading decision on a forecast on some market index. The list goes on. Almost every vertical comes with tons of use cases where AI/ML can be efficiently used in production.

AI/ML processes in production works by 'scoring' models on data in real-time or batch mode to make decisions. Decisions could be:

Representative evaluation and scoring maps for machine learning (ML) training models and testing set. X axis represents the actual diagnosis while the Y axis represents the predicted diagnostic class based on the testing set. (A) Decision forest and decision jungle ML model built to diagnose sensorineural hearing loss (SNHL) compared to conductive hearing loss (CHL) using a 70/30 split. Decision forest is able to diagnose with 100% accuracy while decision jungle is able to diagnose with 80% accuracy. (B) Decision forest, decision jungle, logistic regression, and neural networks ML models built to diagnose SNHL with and without residual hearing. All four ML models were able to diagnose with 100% accuracy.

Difference between Real-time and Batch scoring

Real-time scoring is excellent if you want milli-second response time in making decisions – for example, a retailer is offering recommendations to your users on a website dynamically. Real-time scoring is also instrumental in detecting and flagging fraud or for security when interactions are in-flight. You can even think of real-time scoring in a healthcare environment to detect and alert when medical attention is required. In general, real-time scoring is used where your expert-system should react and trigger downstream processes to mitigate something urgent, that cannot wait.

Batch scoring is useful when we do things like credit risk models and data drift is minimal in transactions arriving in your data lake or warehouse, and scores are considered stationary over a tolerable period. Like sending an email or trigger a customer service call to promote/up-sell/inform or solicit more information from your customer.

Fundamentally, the operational SLAs also drives one of the above. The trade-offs in the scoring environment are also determined by how complex your final model is – like what algorithms were decided to use in scoring + feature engineering effort to transform the incoming data before it's handed off to the algorithms in the pipeline.

Automatic Deployment and Integration with your existing Production systems

The automatic deployment and integration of a AI Models into existing production systems involve several steps to ensure a seamless and efficient transition. Here's a high-level overview of the process:

- Preparation and Training: Train your AI model on the desired task or domain, or use a pre-trained model if available and applicable.
- Containerization: Containerize the models and its dependencies using technologies like Docker. This step helps in ensuring that the model and its environment can be easily deployed to various production environments.
- Orchestration and Deployment: Use container orchestration tools like Kubernetes to manage and deploy the containers efficiently. Kubernetes enables automatic scaling and monitoring.
- API Development: Create an API (Application Programming Interface) for the model. This API should define how your AI model can be interacted with, including input data formats and expected outputs.
- Model Versioning: Implement a versioning system for your models. This ensures that you can easily roll back to previous versions if issues arise with a new model version.
- Testing and Validation: Prior to integration, thoroughly test the Model to ensure that it performs as expected.

Test it against various inputs and edge cases.
- Data Integration: Make sure that the Ai model has access to the necessary data sources, whether that data is stored in databases, external APIs, or other systems. Ensure that data flows smoothly between the models and these sources.
- Security Measures: Implement security measures such as authentication, authorization, and encryption to protect both the Ai Model and the data it interacts with.
- Monitoring and Logging: Set up monitoring and logging to track the performance of the Models in the production environment. This includes monitoring for resource usage, response times, and error rates.
- Scalability: Ensure that your deployment is scalable. Kubernetes, for example, can help with automatic scaling based on traffic.
- Error Handling: Implement robust error-handling mechanisms to gracefully deal with unexpected issues. Define what happens when the model encounters errors and how to alert administrators or support teams.
- Load Balancing: Utilize load balancing to distribute incoming requests across multiple model instances to ensure even load distribution and high availability.
- Integration with Existing Systems: Integrate the Model API with your existing production systems. This may involve modifying existing code or building new components to communicate with the Model.
- Documentation: Create comprehensive documentation for the model API and its integration into the production systems. This documentation should be accessible to developers and operations teams.
- Testing in Production Environment: Before going live, test the entire setup in a production-like environment to uncover any issues that may not have been apparent in a testing or staging environment.
- Deployment to Production: After thorough testing and validation, deploy the model into your production environment.
- Ongoing Monitoring and Maintenance: Continuously monitor the AI model's performance and adjust as needed. Ensure that the system is resilient to failures and can self-recover when possible.

- Feedback Loop: Establish a feedback loop to collect insights from the production usage of the Model. This feedback can be used to fine-tune the model and improve its performance over time.

The automatic deployment and integration of an AI Model into existing production systems is a complex process that requires careful planning, development, and ongoing maintenance. It's essential to have a skilled team with expertise in machine learning, DevOps, and system integration to ensure a successful deployment.

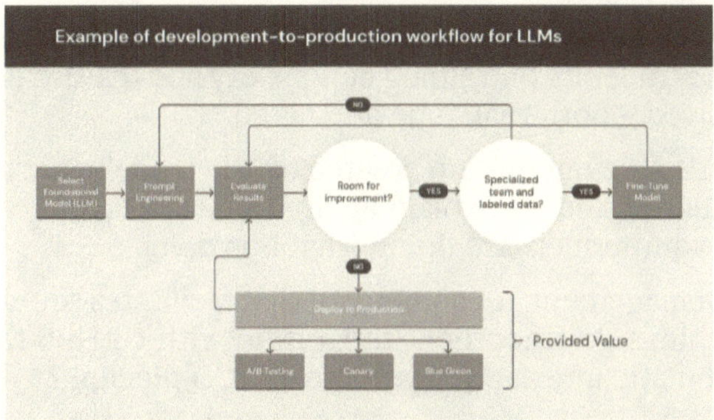

Figure 4.2: *Dev to Prod workflow*

Large language models (LLMs) are a new class of natural language processing (NLP) models that have leaped far ahead of the previous state of the art at a range of tasks, from open question-answering to summarization to following near-arbitrary instructions. The operational requirements of MLOps typically apply to LLMOps as well, but there are challenges with training and deploying LLMs that require a unique approach to LLMOps.

Conclusion

Scoring can't happen without training. You should expect a training setup to support discovering new features, do ultra-fast training with continuous or full learning as new data arrives – without OVERFITTING.

Whatever feature engineering, algorithms, parameters, and ensembles found are packaged inside code artifacts that are portable and moved to production. Portability means deploying to middle-ware, edge systems as well as in-database/in-lake scoring through custom UDFs.

Models are expected to be scored with the best possible SLA given the tradeoffs of training complexity and feature engineering involved – both real-time and batch.

Automatic Documentation created on the models that are being generated for audit + explain ability to business and regulators on why your models are doing what it is doing.

Model management: It's something that facilitates the above and makes things go smoother. Integration with GitHub through a programmatic interface to get into a CICD pipeline?

In next chapter, we will cover

- Enterprise Application for Generative AI
- Challenge for Generative AI Models
- Regulatory Risks and Enterprise concerns
- What it means to create a Responsible AI
- Considerations for Stronger Generative AI

Chapter 5

Content Generation using Generative AI and its authenticity

In today's digitally connected world, content has become the lifeblood of many industries, playing a pivotal role in communication, engagement, and information dissemination. Whether crafting compelling articles, generating product descriptions, creating marketing materials, or even producing art, content is fundamental in establishing a brand's identity, educating consumers, and fostering connections.

With the advent of Generative AI, there has been a seismic shift in how content is generated across various industries. Generative AI models, like GPT-3, have not just revolutionized content creation but have also made a significant impact on a large scale. These models are trained on vast corpora of text, enabling them to generate human-like text, images, and even code with remarkable fluency. As a result, they have swiftly integrated themselves into numerous sectors, presenting solutions to challenges related to scale, efficiency, and personalization.

One essential thing is sometimes forgotten in the middle of all these fast changes: being honest. Being authentic is critical when creating content people can trust and connect with. It helps ensure that what you create feels suitable to your audience, builds trust, and matches your goals. As AI becomes increasingly helpful in creating content, this chapter is about why being authentic is so important.

Why Authenticity Matters

- Authentic content speaks the truth and maintains the integrity of the message.
- It establishes credibility, bolstering the reputation of the content creator.
- Authenticity fosters trust, crucial for building and retaining an audience.
- It aligns content with the creator's values and mission, ensuring consistency.
- In an era of misinformation and deepfakes, authenticity safeguards against deception.

Throughout this chapter, we will delve deep into the world of content generation using Generative AI, exploring how it can both empower and challenge the concept of authenticity. We'll examine real-world use cases, best practices for authenticity, and the ethical considerations surrounding AI-generated content. Ultimately, our goal is to equip you with the knowledge and tools needed to harness the potential of Generative AI in content creation while preserving the authenticity at the core of meaningful communication in the digital age.

The following topics will be covered in this chapter:

- Understanding Content Generation with Generative AI
- The Challenge of Authenticity
- Best Practices for Ensuring Authenticity
- Real-World Use Cases and Examples
- Addressing Social Manipulation and Ethical Considerations

Understanding Content Generation with Generative AI

Generative AI has become a revolutionary aspect in the changing world of technology and content production. It is a class of artificial intelligence models designed to generate human-like content, including text, images, and more. Unlike conventional rule-based systems, these models learn from massive datasets, enabling them to autonomously create contextually relevant and coherent content.

The transformative power of Generative AI is not limited to a single industry. It extends across various sectors, from journalism and marketing to entertainment and beyond. Its ability to automate large-scale content generation tasks has revolutionized how organizations produce and disseminate information. As businesses strive to engage global audiences and stay competitive, staying updated with Generative AI becomes a necessity.

In this chapter, we embark on a journey to explore the inner workings of Generative AI in content generation. We'll delve into the types of content that can be produced, such as articles, product descriptions, creative writing, and even data-driven reports. Through real-world examples and practical insights, we'll unravel how Generative AI reshapes industries by automating tasks, reducing costs, and accelerating content production.

As we delve deeper, we'll also confront the challenges that come with this transformative technology, particularly the issue of authenticity. While Generative AI offers unparalleled efficiency, maintaining authenticity in generated content is a critical concern. We'll discuss the risks associated with misinformation, plagiarism, and ethical considerations, underlining the need for a vigilant and responsible approach.

Following is the list of probable Prompts that you can think of to generate content:

- Generate a product description for a new line of eco-friendly cleaning products.
- Create a short story about a young detective solving a mysterious case in a small town.
- Write an influential article on the importance of mental health awareness.

Types of Content Generated

Generative AI's versatility extends to various content types, making it a versatile and indispensable tool in modern content creation. Among its capabilities, text generation stands as a prominent feature. Generative AI models can craft coherent and contextually relevant textual content across various domains. From news articles to marketing copy and chatbot responses to creative writing, the text generation capacity of these models spans a broad spectrum of applications. In this section, we will explore the types of content generated.

Text Generation

Text generation by Generative AI involves creating human-like textual content autonomously. This content can range from short sentences to lengthy articles, and it can cover diverse topics and writing styles.

`Example`: Consider a marketing company that needs to generate product descriptions for hundreds of items in its online catalog. Instead of hiring a team of writers, they employ Generative AI to produce unique and compelling descriptions for each product.

Consider following the Prompt to generate Textual contents:

- Write a news article about a recent scientific discovery.
- Generate a product description for a new phone.
- Create a short poem about nature.
- Write a conversation between two friends going on a trip.
- Write a short story on a magical adventure.

Image Generation

Generative AI can also create images, illustrations, and visual artwork. These images can be highly detailed and customized to meet specific design needs.

`Example`: An advertising agency seeks to design eye-catching banners for a client's digital marketing campaign. Generative AI is used to generate a series of visually stunning banner designs tailored to the campaign's theme and target audience.

Consider following Prompt for Image generation:

- Generate a series of visually striking banner designs for a digital marketing campaign promoting a new fitness app. The banners should feature vibrant colors, energetic imagery, and motivational slogans to appeal to health-conscious individuals looking to improve their fitness.
- Create eye-catching banner designs for a digital marketing campaign promoting a new line of eco-friendly fashion products. The banners should showcase the products in stylish, environmentally conscious settings, with a focus on sustainability and modern aesthetics.
- Design visually appealing banners for a digital marketing campaign promoting a luxury travel destination. The banners should capture the essence of luxury and relaxation, featuring stunning imagery of the destination's landscapes, accommodations, and activities to entice high-end travelers.

Code Generation

In the realm of software development, Generative AI can generate code snippets, scripts, and even entire applications. This accelerates the coding process and reduces the potential for errors.

Example: A web developer uses Generative AI to automatically generate the HTML and CSS code for a website's user interface based on design mockups. This significantly speeds up the development process.

Consider following prompts to help code generation:

- Create HTML and CSS code for a product landing page based on the provided design. The page should feature a prominent product image, a headline with a call-to-action button, a features section with icons and descriptions, a testimonial section with customer quotes, and a footer with contact information.
- Generate HTML, CSS, and Angular code for a dashboard interface for a financial analytics application. The dashboard should display various financial metrics and charts, such as revenue, expenses, and profit margins. Include interactive elements, such as dropdowns or filters, to allow users to customize their view. The design should be professional and easy to navigate.
- Create ASP.NET MVC code for a registration form for a membership-based website. The form should include fields for username, email, password, and a submit button. Apply form validation to ensure all fields are filled out correctly. The design should be user-friendly and intuitive.

Creative Writing

Generative AI can be employed for creative writing tasks, such as crafting poetry, short stories, or even novel chapters. It can mimic different writing styles and genres.

Example: An aspiring author collaborates with Generative AI to brainstorm and draft plot ideas, character dialogues, and descriptive passages for a science fiction novel.

Consider the following Prompt to ideate creative contents:

- Create a series of engaging anecdotes highlighting our developer's interactions with the AI community. Describe their experiences attending AI conferences, participating in online forums, and collaborating with other developers. Showcase the valuable insights they gain from these interactions and how they use this knowledge to enhance their own understanding and teaching methods.
- Craft a collection of impactful stories showcasing our developer's contributions to the AI community. Describe their efforts to create educational resources, such as blog posts, tutorials, and workshops, to help others learn about AI. Illustrate the impact of their work on the community and how it motivates them to continue sharing their knowledge and inspiring others.
- Develop a compelling story arc for our aspiring developer's journey into the world of AI. Start with a captivating introduction that sets the stage for their fascination with AI. Describe their early experiences, the challenges they face, and the pivotal moments that drive their passion to master AI and share their knowledge with others.

Data Reports and Insights:

Generative AI can assist in generating data-driven reports, research summaries, and analytical insights. It can process large datasets and extract meaningful information.

Example: A financial institution uses Generative AI to analyze market data and generate daily reports on stock performance, economic trends, and investment recommendations.

These examples illustrate the breadth of Generative AI's capabilities and its potential to transform content generation across industries. As we explore further in this chapter, we will dive deeper into each type of content generation, examining practical use cases and the implications of harnessing Generative AI for these purposes.

The Challenge of Authenticity

Authenticity is a central concern in content creation, and with the integration of Generative AI, it has taken on new dimensions and challenges. This section dives into the complexities of authenticity and why it's a critical consideration when utilizing Generative AI for content generation.

Authenticity in Content

- Defining Authenticity: Authenticity, in the context of content creation, refers to the quality of being genuine, original, and true to its intended purpose or source. It signifies that the content accurately represents the values, voice, and intentions of its creator. Authentic content is free from deception, manipulation, or misrepresentation.
- Importance of Authenticity: Maintaining authenticity is paramount because it builds trust between content creators and their audiences. Authentic content resonates with readers, viewers, or users because it reflects sincerity and reliability. Authenticity helps establish credibility, fosters long-term relationships, and ensures that the content aligns with the creator's objectives and values.

Risks and Concerns

While Generative AI offers numerous advantages in content generation, it introduces specific risks and concerns:

- Plagiarism: Generative AI can inadvertently produce content that closely resembles existing works, leading to accusations of plagiarism. This can harm the reputation of the content creator and lead to legal issues.
- Misinformation: AI-generated content may inadvertently disseminate false or misleading information if the training data contains inaccuracies or biases. This can misinform readers and damage trust in the content.
- Ethical Issues: Generative AI can be used unethically to create deceptive content, including fake news, deepfakes, or malicious narratives. Such misuse can have far-reaching consequences, including social unrest and harm to individu-

als and organizations.

Concerns about Bias

Generative AI models can inherit biases present in their training data, leading to biased or discriminatory content. This raises concerns about fairness and equity in content creation.

Lack of Human Judgment

AI lacks the moral and ethical judgment that humans possess. It may generate content that, while technically accurate, could be considered insensitive or offensive.

Navigating the challenge of authenticity in the context of Generative AI-driven content creation requires careful consideration, ethical guidelines, and a commitment to maintaining the trust of the audience. In the subsequent sections of this chapter, we will explore best practices and strategies to address these risks and ensure that AI-generated content upholds the values of authenticity and ethical integrity.

Best Practices for Ensuring Authenticity

Authenticity in content creation is paramount for building trust and credibility. To ensure authenticity, creators should strive to provide accurate information, cite reputable sources, and use a tone that resonates with their audience. Transparency about any biases or conflicts of interest is essential, as is maintaining a consistent voice and style throughout the content. Engaging with the audience and responding to feedback can also help foster authenticity. Ultimately, authenticity is about being genuine and honest in your communication, which builds trust and establishes a meaningful connection with your audience.

In this section, we will put a light on the Bets practices.

Training Data and Fine-Tuning

The quality of training data plays an important role in determining the authenticity of generated content in AI systems. Training data teaches AI models how to generate text, images, or other forms of content that mimic human-created content. If the training data is of good quality, the AI model may learn correct patterns or produce outputs consistent with human standards, leading to inauthentic content.

One key aspect of training data quality is its relevance to the task. For example, if the goal is to generate news articles, the training data should consist of high-quality, factually accurate news articles. Using unrelated or low-quality training data can result in the AI model producing misleading or irrelevant content.

Another critical factor is the diversity of the training data. AI models benefit from exposure to a wide range of examples to learn the nuances of language and style. If the training data is narrower or homogeneous, the AI model may produce content that needs more creativity and originality, leading to inauthentic outputs.

Furthermore, the accuracy and consistency of the training data are crucial. Inconsistencies or errors in the training data can confuse the AI model and result in inconsistent or illogical outputs. For example, if the training data contains conflicting information about a topic, the AI model may need help generating coherent content.

Additionally, the training data size can also impact the authenticity of the generated content. Generally, larger training datasets provide more examples for the AI model to learn from, resulting in more accurate and nuanced outputs. However, simply increasing the size of the training data is only sometimes the solution; the quality of the data remains paramount.

It's also important to consider the bias present in the training data. It's the training data on which AI models are trained, so if the training data contains bias, the AI model may replicate and even amplify that bias in its outputs. This can lead to inauthentic content that reflects and perpetuates harmful stereotypes or misinformation.

Fine-tuning models is crucial for ensuring that the generated content aligns with specific authenticity requirements. In the context of generative AI, fine-tuning refers to adjusting a pre-trained model to suit a particular task or domain better. This process is essential for achieving more accurate and relevant output, especially when the goal is to create content that resonates with a specific audience or meets certain quality standards.

One key reason for fine-tuning models is to enhance the authenticity of the generated content. Authenticity in this context refers to the extent to which the content feels genuine, reliable, and consistent with the desired tone, style, and context. For example, fine-tuning natural language generation tasks can help ensure that the language used is appropriate for the intended audience, the information presented is accurate, and the overall tone matches the desired voice or brand image.

Fine-tuning can also help address issues related to bias and fairness in AI-generated content. By training the model on a more diverse and representative dataset, developers can reduce the risk of generating biased or discriminatory content. This is particularly important in applications where the content may impact individuals or communities, such as news reporting, customer service, or educational materials.

Another critical aspect of fine-tuning is its role in improving the fluency and coherence of the generated content. By fine-tuning the model on specific language patterns and structures relevant to the task, developers can ensure that the generated content flows naturally and is easily understood. This is essential for creating engaging and informative content that communicates the intended message effectively.

In addition to enhancing authenticity, fine-tuning models can also improve the efficiency and effectiveness of content generation. By focusing the model's training on a specific task or domain, developers can reduce the time and computational resources required to generate high-quality content. This can be particularly beneficial in real-time or resource-constrained applications, where speed and efficiency are paramount.

Human-in-the Loop

The concept of "human-in-the-loop" is all about combining the strengths of humans and machines. In content generation, humans are involved alongside AI or other automated systems.

Here's how it works: First, the AI or machine does its job, like generating text or creating designs. Then, a human steps in to review and improve the content. This human touch is not just important; it's invaluable. It adds a unique blend of creativity, context, and quality control that machines simply can't replicate, making your role in the process essential.

In content generation, the human-in-the-loop approach ensures that the final output meets the desired standards and aligns with the brand's voice and goals. It also allows for more personalized and engaging content, as humans can add a unique perspective and tailor it to specific audiences.

The human-in-the-loop approach is particularly valuable in dealing with complex or sensitive topics, where human judgment and understanding are irreplaceable. For instance, in medical or legal content, a human's involvement is essential to ensure accuracy and compliance with regulations.

Human oversight plays a crucial role in enhancing authenticity in various areas. In content creation, human oversight is the bedrock of credibility. It ensures that the content is accurate, relevant, and resonates with the intended audience. For example, a human editor can review an article to ensure that the information presented is factually correct and free from errors. This way, human oversight not only maintains but strengthens the credibility and authenticity of the content, instilling trust in your audience.

Human oversight is essential for providing personalized and empathetic support in customer service. For instance, a customer service representative can listen to their concerns, empathize with their situation, and provide a tailored solution. This human touch enhances the authenticity of the interaction, making the customer feel valued and understood.

In AI, human oversight is crucial for ensuring that AI systems are fair, unbiased, and ethical. For example, human reviewers can evaluate the output of AI algorithms to identify and correct any biases or errors. This oversight helps ensure that the AI system behaves in a way consistent with human values and norms, enhancing its authenticity and trustworthiness.

Addressing Social Manipulation and Ethical Considerations

Social manipulation has become a pressing concern in today's digital age, with widespread implications for individuals, societies, and democracies. Social media platforms, in particular, have been implicated in spreading misinformation, manipulating public opinion, and influencing elections. Addressing social manipulation requires a multifaceted approach that considers both technological and ethical considerations.

Technological advancements, such as artificial intelligence and big data analytics, have enabled sophisticated forms of social manipulation. These technologies can target individuals with personalized content, exploit cognitive biases, and amplify divisive narratives. As a result, individuals may be unknowingly exposed to false information or manipulated into taking actions that serve the interests of others.

Ethical considerations play a crucial role in addressing social manipulation. It is essential to consider the impact of technological interventions on individuals' autonomy, privacy, and well-being. Moreover, there are broader ethical questions regarding the role of technology companies and governments in regulating and mitigating social manipulation. It is imperative to ensure that any interventions are ethically justified and aligned with democratic principles.

One approach to addressing social manipulation is through increased transparency and accountability. Technology companies can be more transparent about their algorithms, data practices, and content moderation policies. This transparency can help build trust with users and enable independent scrutiny of their practices.

Another approach is empowering individuals to make informed decisions about their content. This can be achieved through media literacy programs that teach individuals to evaluate information and identify misinformation critically. By equipping individuals with these skills, they can better protect themselves from social manipulation.

Regulatory frameworks can also play a crucial role in addressing social manipulation. Governments can enact laws and regulations that require transparency from technology companies and prohibit deceptive practices. Additionally, regulatory agencies can enforce these laws and hold companies accountable for violations.

Social Manipulation

Exploring the dangers of social manipulation through AI-generated content is crucial in understanding the potential risks that could impact individuals and society. Social manipulation is influencing people's thoughts, behaviors, and decisions through deceptive or misleading tactics. With the rise of AI technology, particularly in content generation, these risks have become more prevalent and concerning.

AI-generated content refers to articles, videos, or images created or manipulated by artificial intelligence. While AI has the potential to revolutionize content creation and improve efficiency, it also presents significant risks when used maliciously or irresponsibly.

One of the primary risks of AI-generated content is the spread of misinformation and fake news. AI can create compelling and realistic content that is difficult to distinguish from genuine information. This can lead to the dissemination of false information, which can have serious consequences, such as influencing public opinion, spreading fear and panic, and undermining trust in reliable sources of information.

Another risk is manipulating public opinion and behavior. AI can be used to create targeted content designed to manipulate people's emotions, beliefs, and actions. This can be used for political purposes, such as influencing elections or promoting extremist ideologies, as well as for commercial purposes, such as marketing and advertising.

AI-generated content also poses risks to privacy and security. AI algorithms can analyze vast amounts of data to create personalized content tailored to individual preferences and behaviors. While this can enhance user experience, it also raises concerns about data privacy and the potential for misuse of personal information.

Furthermore, AI-generated content can have unintended consequences, such as reinforcing stereotypes, spreading harmful ideologies, or promoting unethical behavior. This highlights the importance of responsible AI development and usage to mitigate these risks.

To address these risks, it is essential to implement safeguards and regulations that ensure AI-generated content is used responsibly and ethically. This includes ensuring transparency and accountability in AI development and usage and promoting media literacy and critical thinking skills to help individuals identify and mitigate the impact of social manipulation.

Followings are some real-world examples of social manipulation:

- **Fake News on Social Media**: People spread false information on social media platforms, like Facebook and Twitter, to mislead others and influence their opinions. For example, during elections, fake news articles might make people believe untrue things about candidates to change how they vote.
- **Manipulative Ads**: Companies use targeted ads online to show people products or ideas based on their personal information, like age or interests. For instance, a company might use data from someone's internet searches to show ads for products they think they want, even if they don't need them.
- **Bot Accounts**: Some people use automated accounts bots, to spread messages or comments on social media. These bots can make it seem like many people agree with a specific idea or support a particular cause, even if it's not true. For instance, bot accounts might post positive comments about a product to make it seem more popular than it is.
- **Filter Bubbles**: Social media algorithms show people content they're likely to agree with based on past behavior. This can create a "filter bubble," where people only see information aligning with their beliefs. For example, if someone only interacts with posts from a specific political party, they might never see viewpoints from the other side, leading them to believe everyone agrees with them.
- **Disinformation Campaigns**: Governments or organizations spread false information to confuse or manipulate people. For example, a country might use disinformation to create distrust in another country's government or influence public opinion on important issues like healthcare or climate change.

These examples also refer to social manipulation, which can take various forms, including spreading fake news and using targeted ads based on personal data. These tactics can influence people's beliefs, opinions, and behaviors, highlighting the need for critical thinking and awareness when consuming information online.

Security and Privacy by Design

Artificial intelligence (AI) offers many benefits, but it also has risks, especially in terms of security and privacy. To mitigate these risks, several strategies can be implemented.

Firstly, it is crucial to ensure that AI systems are built with security in mind from the beginning. This includes implementing strong authentication and access controls to prevent unauthorized access to sensitive data. Data encryption should also be used to protect data at rest and in transit.

Another essential strategy is regularly updating and patching AI systems to protect against known vulnerabilities. This helps to ensure that the system is protected against the latest threats. Furthermore, conducting regular security audits and penetration testing can help identify and address potential security issues before they can be exploited.

In terms of privacy considerations, it's important to implement data minimization practices, which involve only collecting and storing the data necessary for the AI system to function. Additionally, privacy-enhancing technologies such as differential privacy can help protect sensitive data by adding noise to prevent individual data points from being identified.

Transparency is also key in mitigating privacy risks. AI systems should be designed so that their decisions can be explained and understood by users. This can help build trust and ensure users know how their data is used.

Finally, it's important to establish clear policies and guidelines for using AI systems, especially in sensitive areas such as healthcare or finance. These policies should outline how data will be collected, used, and protected and should be regularly reviewed and updated to reflect changing regulations and best practices.

The Importance of Embedding Principles into AI Models

Embedding principles into artificial intelligence (AI) models ensures these technologies are developed and used responsibly. These principles, which include ethics, transparency, fairness, and accountability, are essential for building trust in AI systems and ensuring that they benefit society.

Ethics is one of the fundamental principles that should be embedded into AI models. Ethics in AI involves ensuring that AI systems are developed and used in a morally acceptable way. This includes respecting the rights and dignity of individuals, avoiding harm, and promoting the greater good. Embedding ethical principles into AI models helps ensure that these technologies are used in a fair and just way.

Transparency is another important principle that should be embedded into AI models. Transparency involves ensuring that AI systems are understandable and explainable. This is important because it helps build trust in AI systems and allows users to understand how they make decisions. For example, in the case of a self-driving car, the car needs to be able to explain why it made a particular decision, such as braking or swerving, to ensure the safety of its passengers and others on the road.

Fairness is also a crucial principle that should be embedded into AI models. Fairness in AI involves ensuring that AI systems do not discriminate against individuals or groups of people. This is important because AI systems can perpetuate existing biases and inequalities if incorrectly designed and implemented. For example, a biased recruitment AI system against certain demographic groups could lead to discriminatory hiring practices.

Accountability is another fundamental principle that should be embedded into AI models. Accountability involves ensuring that individuals and organizations are held responsible for the decisions and actions of AI systems. This is important because it helps ensure that AI systems are used responsibly and that those who are harmed by them have recourse.

For example, if an AI system is used to make decisions about healthcare treatment, it is important for the system's developers to be held accountable if the system makes a mistake that harms a patient.

Conclusion

In this chapter, we have understood that content generation using generative AI offers many benefits but raises important questions about authenticity. While AI can create indistinguishable content from human-generated content, ensuring that this content is authentic is essential.

Authenticity in AI-generated content means that it resonates with the audience, builds trust, and aligns with the values and objectives of the creator. This is important because authenticity is key to engaging and retaining an audience.

To ensure authenticity in AI-generated content, creators can take several steps:

- They can provide input and guidance to the AI system, helping to shape the content to align with their vision and goals.
- They can use AI tools to analyze the content and ensure brand voice and style consistency.
- They can engage with their audience to gather feedback and adjust the content.

By taking these steps, creators can ensure that their AI-generated content is authentic and resonates with their audience. This not only helps to build trust and credibility but also enhances the overall impact of the content.

The next chapter will discuss Ethical AI, its impact, and various legal aspects.

JOIN US ON THE ARCCHIE PUBLICATIONS DISCORD SERVER

Connect with fellow readers, authors, and enthusiasts to discuss all things related to our publications and the exciting world of AI, programming, and learning. Share your insights, ask questions, and engage in vibrant discussions to expand your knowledge and inspire creativity. Take advantage of this opportunity to be part of a dynamic community dedicated to exploring the frontiers of technology and innovation. Join our Discord Server today and be part of the ARCCHIE PUBLICATIONS community!

Chapter 6

Ethical AI – Discussion of Legal aspects on Generative AI

Today, businesses are actively exploring the potential of generative AI, engaging in use case identification, conducting proof-of-value exercises, executing pilots, and integrating the technology into their operational processes. ChatGPT and other generative AI technologies are extremely powerful and can be used for many purposes, but at the same time give rise to significant legal and ethical issues.

Ethical considerations in the development and use of artificial intelligence (AI) have become increasingly important as AI technologies have advanced. In the early days of AI research, ethical considerations were not at the forefront.

Researchers focused on creating AI systems that could solve problems and perform tasks, largely unaware of the potential ethical implications. During this period, AI research faced funding cuts and a loss of interest due to unmet expectations. Ethical considerations played a minor role, as the field grappled with more immediate challenges.

As AI applications became more pervasive, ethical concerns surrounding AI gained prominence. Issues such as bias in algorithms, privacy violations, and the potential for AI to exacerbate inequality were widely discussed.

Leading AI organizations, including OpenAI, began to develop guidelines and principles for ethical AI. OpenAI, for instance, released its "AI Principles," emphasizing the importance of ensuring AI benefits all of humanity.

Ongoing: Ethical AI in Practice

Today, ethical AI is a central concern in the AI community. Researchers and organizations are actively working to minimize biases, ensure transparency, and address the societal impact of AI.

Ethical AI guidelines, standards, and regulations are expected to continue evolving as AI technologies advance.

The history of ethical AI reflects the growing awareness of the importance of ethical considerations in AI development and deployment. As AI becomes more integrated into society, addressing ethical issues will remain a critical aspect of AI research and practice.

Discussing Privacy

Privacy of the person, privacy of behavior and action, privacy of personal communication, privacy of data and image, privacy of thoughts and feelings, privacy of location and space, and privacy of association (including group privacy).

Internal - General Use Analysis of personal data through AI systems can lead to significant harms. AI is by far not the only threat to privacy, but it adds new capabilities that can either exacerbate existing threats, for example by automating mass surveillance based on biometric data.

AI privacy, also known as AI data privacy or privacy in the context of artificial intelligence, refers to the protection of individuals' personal data and the safeguarding of their privacy rights in the age of AI. It involves ensuring that AI systems and applications respect and adhere to privacy principles and regulations while processing and analyzing data.

Here are some key aspects of AI privacy:

- **Data Protection**: AI systems often rely on vast amounts of data to function effectively. AI privacy involves protecting this data, especially when it includes sensitive personal information.
- **Informed Consent**: Users should be informed about how their data is being collected and used by AI systems. Obtaining informed consent is a fundamental aspect of AI privacy.
- **Data Minimization**: AI applications should collect and retain only the data necessary for their intended purposes, minimizing the risk of unauthorized access or misuse.
- **Data Anonymization and Pseudonymization**: Personal data should be anonymized or pseudonymized to reduce the risk of re-identification and to protect user privacy.
- **Transparency**: AI systems should be transparent in their operations. Users and data subjects should understand how decisions are made and whether AI is involved in those decisions.

- **Algorithmic Fairness**: AI systems must avoid biases that could lead to discrimination. Ensuring that algorithms are fair and do not unfairly impact certain groups is a privacy concern.
- **Data Security**: Protecting data against breaches and unauthorized access is essential for AI privacy. Strong data security measures must be in place.
- **User Control**: Users should have control over their data. They should be able to access, correct, and delete their data, as well as opt out of data processing where possible.
- **Compliance with Regulations**: AI developers and organizations should adhere to data privacy regulations such as the General Data Protection Regulation (GDPR) in Europe and similar laws in other regions.
- **Ethical Use of Data**: Organizations should use AI in ways that respect ethical principles, such as respecting human rights, avoiding surveillance, and not exploiting data for unintended or harmful purposes.
- **Privacy by Design**: AI systems should incorporate privacy protections from the outset of development, rather than as an afterthought.

AI privacy is crucial because AI systems often process vast amounts of data, and privacy violations can have significant consequences, including identity theft, discrimination, surveillance, and breaches of personal and confidential information. Protecting privacy in AI is not only a legal requirement but also an ethical responsibility that helps build trust with users and the public at large. It is an ongoing challenge as AI technology continues to advance and as privacy regulations evolve.

Common Enterprise Applications for Generative AI

There are four broad areas in which generative AI finds application within enterprises:

Enterprise virtual assistants and knowledge search

This encompasses use cases such as question-and-answering, intelligent search and summarization on enterprise documents. The aim is to enhance customer experience, drive employee productivity and accelerate research and development.

Content generation for digital commerce and media

Generative AI can be harnessed to develop digital marketing accelerators for adaptive storytelling, generate dynamic digital avatars with natural speech interactions, generate scripts and images for advertisements, create conversational interfaces for digital commerce, and perform content generation across various media channels.

Acceleration in software development lifecycle

Generative AI is considered as a transformative technology for accelerating software development processes by assisting in code generation, converting legacy code for migration purposes, generating documentation and test cases, and providing aid in software incident management.

Synthetic data generation

Many analyst firms are predicting that large proportion of digital data will be AI generated. Most of that data will be used for training AI models. This entails using generative AI to create synthetic data when real data is either unavailable or inaccessible due to regulatory constraints or real data doesn't have required variations. Generative AI facilitates data anonymization to address privacy and security requirements and enable the simulation of environments such as digital twins and the metaverse.

Challenges for Generative AI Models

Key questions CISOs are asking: Who is using the technology in my organization, and for what purpose? How can I protect enterprise information (data) when employees are interacting with GenAI? How can I manage the security risks of the underlying technology? How do I balance the security tradeoffs with the value the technology offers? This document provides information on risks and suggested best practices that security teams and CISOs can leverage within their own organizations and serves as a call to action for the community to evangelize and further engage on the topic.

From a legal and regulatory perspective, the recent enactment of India's Digital Personal Data Protection Act inspired the country's government to kick-start its compliance journey. Furthermore, in 2022, the Indian government proposed enacting the Digital India Act to provide contemporaneous legal standards catering to the country's evolving digital ecosystem. Given its widespread use in critical fields such as health care, banking and aviation, this proposed law seeks to regulate AI.

Generative AI – Regulatory Risks and Enterprise Concerns

Legal Basis of Data Collection	• One of the primary causes of regulatory actions across EU, Australia, Canada. • Legal basis is required for the collection, storage and processing of public data as per EU General Data Protection Regulation and proposed European AI Act. • Potential liability of data scraped from web or personal information that may have been used for model training, this might lead to potential violation of California Consumer Privacy Act and California Privacy Rights Act.
Transparency	• Lack of explainability of responses generated • Lack of transparency on data sources for training of models • No information to individuals on how their data is used to train models
Copyright Infringement	• Potential use of copyrighted information in training models, leading to copyright violations in generated responses. https://www.infoq.com/news/2022/11/lawsuit-github-copilot/
Inaccurate Results	• Wrong answers • Hallucination – generation of highly plausible but incorrect responses

Information Security Violation	• Leakage of confidential information by employees using ChatGPT
	https://in.mashable.com/tech/50407/whoops-samsung-workers-accidentally-leaked-trade-secrets-via-chatgpt
Inappropriate Content	• Lack of age verification • Vulnerability to jailbreaks to generate inappropriate responses

AI is one of the most powerful technologies of our time, with broad applications. President Biden has been clear that to seize the opportunities AI presents, we must first manage its risks. To that end, the Administration has taken significant action to promote responsible AI innovation that places people, communities, and the public good at the center, and manages risks to individuals and our society, security, and economy. This includes the landmark Blueprint for an AI Bill of Rights and related executive actions, the AI Risk Management Framework, a roadmap for standing up a National AI Research Resource, active work to address the national security concerns raised by AI, as well as investments and actions announced earlier this month. Last week, the Administration also convened representatives from leading AI companies for a briefing from experts across the national security community on cyber threats to AI systems and best practices to secure high-value networks and information.

Key Considerations a Stronger Generative AI Approach

Understanding the range of potential GenAI risks, threats, and impacts in an enterprise setting has become a priority, and must be carefully considered. These can be broken down to technological or process extensions of existing risks, legal and regulatory risks, and some risks that are completely new. To provide an overview of these risks, we created the reference table below, arranged and prioritized by risk level, current as of

April 2023 (Disclaimer: Every organization is unique, these are offered as guidelines). Enterprises can take proactive measures to minimize the potential negative impact of GenAI usage and ensure that they are leveraging this powerful tool in a secure, compliant, and responsible manner.

To develop a stronger generative AI approach, you should consider various factors related to model architecture, data, training, and application. Here are key considerations:

Model Size and Complexity:

Large-scale models with more parameters tend to perform better in many tasks, but they also require substantial computational resources. Evaluate the trade-off between model size and practicality for your specific application.

Training Data Quality and Quantity:

High-quality and diverse training data are essential. Ensure that the data is representative of the task you're addressing and free from biases that might affect model performance.

Data Preprocessing:

Proper preprocessing of training data, such as data cleaning, normalization, and feature engineering, can significantly impact model effectiveness.

Transfer Learning:

Leverage pre-trained models or transfer learning to build on existing knowledge and fine-tune models for specific tasks. This can save time and resources.

Data Augmentation:

Use data augmentation techniques to generate additional training data and improve the model's ability to generalize.

Model Evaluation

Define clear evaluation metrics and use appropriate benchmarks to assess the model's performance. Consider human evaluations, objective metrics, and task-specific criteria.

Bias Mitigation

Implement strategies to identify and mitigate biases in the training data and model output. Fairness, equity, and ethical considerations are critical.

Data Privacy and Security

Ensure that sensitive information is adequately protected, and adhere to data privacy regulations. Encrypt and secure data during training and deployment.

Control and Fine-Tuning

Develop methods for controlling the output of the model, such as guidelines, filtering, or rule-based post-processing to align the generated content with desired criteria.

Interpretability and Explainability

Enhance the model's interpretability and explainability to provide insight into its decision-making process. This is particularly important in critical applications.

Model Robustness

Make the model more robust against adversarial attacks and perturbations. Consider techniques like adversarial training and input sanitization.

Sustainability:

Explore energy-efficient training and deployment methods to reduce the environmental impact of large models.

Customization and Personalization

Develop strategies to enable customization and personalization while respecting privacy and ethical boundaries.

Deployment Infrastructure

Design efficient and scalable deployment infrastructure to ensure that the model can be used in real-world applications without significant latency.

Regulatory Compliance

Stay informed about AI regulations and ensure compliance with data privacy and ethical guidelines.

Feedback Loops

Establish feedback loops to continuously improve the model by collecting user feedback and monitoring its performance in real-world scenarios.

Ethical Considerations

Ethical considerations should be an integral part of the AI development process. Develop and adhere to ethical guidelines and principles.

User Education and Guidelines

Educate users about the capabilities and limitations of the AI model and provide clear guidelines for responsible usage.

Stakeholder Collaboration

Collaborate with relevant stakeholders, including domain experts, ethicists, and regulators, to ensure a well-rounded approach.

Continual Research and Development

Stay updated on the latest research and advancements in AI to incorporate the best practices and methodologies.

A strong generative AI approach involves a combination of technical, ethical, and practical considerations. It's essential to strike a balance between model performance and ethical, privacy, and societal considerations when developing and deploying generative AI models.

While these broad principles can help mitigate many of the risks associated with generative AI in an enterprise setting, their applicability varies depending on the use case. For example, a virtual assistant used by employees will have higher adaptability for custom training, thus presenting relatively lower risks when implemented alongside the other principles. On the other hand, a marketing catchphrase generator or code generator relies more on the pre-trained knowledge of the model and therefore has a higher propensity of generating plagiarized or copyrighted content.

Businesses should conduct a risk assessment for each individual use case, considering the applicability of these principles, to determine their roadmap of adapting generative AI based on the specific risk profile of each use case.

Should We Pause Giant AI Experiments?

John Behrens, University of Notre Dame professor of the practice of digital learning and director of the Idzik Computing & Digital Technologies Program, told CMSWire that prominent AI technologists, as well as industry leaders such as Elon Musk, are concerned that we've "let the genie out of the bottle" and do not sufficiently understand either how the new AI systems will behave or how humans behave when interacting with them.

"We are seeing a lot of unpredictable behavior in both computer systems and humans that may or may not be safe, and these voices are arguing we need time to understand what we've gotten ourselves into before we make more systems that humans are apt to inappropriately use," said Behrens.

Behrens is referring to a petition from the Future of Life Institute published last month requesting that all of the current AI labs immediately pause the development of any AI past GPT-4. As of April 10, the petition had 18,980 signatures including Yoshua Bengio, founder and scientific director at the Montreal Institute of Learning Algorithms; Stuart Russell, Berkeley professor of computer science and director of the Center for Intelligent Systems; Musk, CEO of SpaceX, Tesla and Twitter; and Steve Wozniak, co-founder of Apple.

The open letter, as it's being called, reflects upon concerns that generative AI could potentially "flood our information channels with propaganda and untruth " and that there is the potential that we risk "loss of control of our civilization." The petition goes on to demand an immediate pause on AI development, and if that isn't agreed upon, asks for government intervention:

"Therefore, we call on all AI labs to immediately pause for at least 6 months the training of AI systems more powerful than GPT-4. If such a pause cannot be enacted quickly, governments should step in and institute a moratorium."

The Ethics and Morality of Generative AI

Since OpenAI announced its ChatGPT large language model generative AI chat application, Microsoft announced the new AI-driven Bing, and Google announced its generative AI-driven Bard, the public has been continually trying to engage these AI models in conversations that show they are sentient, that they have feelings and desires, and that they can be biased or malicious toward their creators and users.

How should we approach AI governance and risk management?

If used well, AI has the potential to make organisations more efficient, effective and innovative. However, AI also raises significant risks for the rights and freedoms of individuals, as well as compliance challenges for organisations.

Different technological approaches will either exacerbate or mitigate some of these issues, but many others are much broader than the specific technology. As the rest of this guidance suggests, the data protection implications of AI are heavily dependent on the specific use cases, the population they are deployed on, other overlapping regulatory requirements, as well as social, cultural and political considerations.

While AI increases the importance of embedding data protection by design and default into an organisation's culture and processes, the technical complexities of AI systems can make this more difficult. Demonstrating how you have addressed these complexities is an important element of accountability.

You cannot delegate these issues to data scientists or engineering teams. Your senior management, including DPOs, are also accountable for understanding and addressing them appropriately and promptly (although overall accountability for data protection compliance lies with the controller, ie your organisation).

To do so, in addition to their own upskilling, your senior management will need diverse, well-resourced teams to support them in carrying out their responsibilities. You also need to align your internal structures, roles and responsibilities maps, training requirements, policies and incentives to your overall AI governance and risk management strategy.

It is important that you do not underestimate the initial and ongoing level of investment of resources and effort that is required. You must be able to demonstrate, on an ongoing basis, how you have addressed data protection by design and default obligations. Your governance and risk management capabilities need to be proportionate to your use of AI. This is particularly true now while AI adoption is still in its initial stages, and the technology itself, as well as the associated laws, regulations, governance and risk management best practices are developing quickly.

Growing Drumbeat Over Copyright Concerns

Much of the early public concern about AI chatbots deals with the question of copyright violation. Specifically, when the chatbot is asked to write text on a specific topic, and it reaches out to the Internet for information in order to compose that text, might it be violating copyright with something that it "grabs?"

Chatbot such as ChatGPT doesn't grab entire chapters, sections or even passages of text. Instead, it "builds" a narrative one word at a time, looking for the most common word it finds in use for each point in the narrative, and for the exact placement of words in the text.

In that sense, ChatGPT writes the absolute "most average" text possible for any topic, Wang said. But that is not how humans think or write. He, therefore, discounts the likelihood that an organization needs to fear copyright violation.

Organizations Should Always Use Care When Privacy and Security Are at Risk

Confirming the need for caution is Alberto Roldan, a well-known business strategist and AI expert who has extensive experience in the field and is the author of a weekly newsletter on AI strategies.

"Organizations should be cautious about using AI in areas where data privacy and security, such as handling sensitive personal or financial information," Roldan said. "It is important to ensure that AI systems are designed and implemented in a way that protects customer data and meets regulatory requirements."

If there is good news on this front, it is that ChatGPT is still in its infancy, and fears over potentially bad behavior may be exaggerated — at the moment, Gao said.

"AI is getting better through improvement both from a vendor perspective and more widespread use," explained Jason James, a former healthcare chief information officer (CIO) and current technology adviser. "In order for AI to be effective, it must have not only better programming but greater data sets in order to analyze and learn. The more it gets used, the more it learns and adapts. Much like young children, wisdom comes through experience. One expected that the greater number of experiences allow for greater understanding of human behavior."

The growth of generative artificial intelligence and its legal issues

The story so far: Artificial intelligence (AI) is making advancements globally even as governments struggle to establish a regulatory framework for the evolving technology. Joining the global efforts to govern AI, United States President Joe Biden last month issued an executive order to promote the "safe, se-cure, and trustworthy" use and development of AI by addressing broad issues related to privacy, misinformation and discrimina-tion.

The order, signed by Mr. Biden on October 30 2023, lays down a preliminary set of guidelines for American companies and fed-eral agencies to follow when dealing with the design, acquisi-tion and deployment of advanced AI systems, with security as its core, and before making such technologies available to the public. Mr. Biden has insisted that the order is the "most signif-icant action" any government in the world has ever taken on AI safety, and also called upon the Congress to pass bipartisan leg-islation to stop Big Tech platforms from collecting the personal data of citizens.

Generative artificial intelligence (AI) has witnessed significant growth and advancement in recent years, but this growth has also brought about various legal and ethical challenges. Here's an overview of the growth of generative AI and the associated legal issues:

Growth of Generative AI:

- Advancements in Models: The development of large-scale generative models like GPT-3, GPT-4, and similar models has led to impressive capabilities in natural language generation, image synthesis, and more.
- Diverse Applications: Generative AI has found applications in diverse domains, including content generation, chatbots, art generation, code generation, and more.
- Commercial Adoption: Many businesses and organizations are integrating generative AI into their products and services for various purposes, including content creation, customer support, and data analysis.
- Research and Innovation: AI research in generative models continues to expand, with a focus on improving model per-formance and addressing limitations.

Legal Issues Associated with Generative AI:

- Intellectual Property: Generative AI can create content that raises questions about copyright and intellectual property. Determining ownership of AI-generated content can be challenging.
- Data Privacy: The use of AI for data analysis and generation may raise concerns about privacy, especially when AI systems handle sensitive or personal data.
- Bias and Discrimination: AI models, if not properly trained, can produce biased or discriminatory content. This raises concerns about potential legal ramifications and regulatory compliance.
- Regulatory Compliance: Generative AI usage must adhere to various data protection and privacy regulations, such as GDPR in Europe. Violations can result in legal consequences.
- Misinformation and Disinformation: The widespread use of AI for generating content increases the risk of misinformation and disinformation. Legal issues may arise if AI-generated content spreads false or harmful information.
- Content Moderation: Platforms that use generative AI must implement robust content moderation systems to prevent the dissemination of harmful, illegal, or inappropriate content.
- Cybersecurity and Hacking: The security of generative AI models and data used for training is crucial to prevent hacking, data breaches, and malicious use.
- Ethical Concerns: Ethical issues, such as deepfakes and the manipulation of images and videos, have legal implications, including potential criminal consequences.
- Liability: Determining liability for AI-generated content or actions can be complex. It may involve questions of responsibility, accountability, and the role of developers, users, and AI systems.
- User Consent: Users interacting with generative AI systems may need to provide informed consent, particularly when their data or interactions are used for training or generating content.
- Consumer Protection: Ensuring that AI-generated products and services meet quality standards and consumer expectations is vital for legal compliance.
- International Regulations: AI development and usage are

subject to varying regulations in different countries, making it challenging to navigate a global legal landscape.

The growth of generative AI offers substantial benefits, but it also introduces complex legal considerations. As a result, policymakers, lawmakers, and legal experts are working to develop frameworks and regulations to address these legal issues while

fostering responsible and ethical AI deployment.

Transparency in AI systems and how to limit potential biases in AI models

Transparency in AI systems is essential for building trust, understanding decision-making processes, and identifying and mitigating potential biases.

To ensure transparency and limit biases in AI models, consider the following best practices:

Data Collection and Preparation

- Use diverse and representative datasets: Ensure your training data is comprehensive and reflects the diversity of the population. Biased data can lead to biased models.
- Label data carefully: Pay attention to how data is labeled and annotated to avoid introducing bias. Review labels for potential bias in training data.

Preprocessing and Data Cleaning

- Detect and correct bias: Implement data preprocessing techniques to identify and mitigate biases in training data.
- Address data imbalances: Ensure that underrepresented groups are not disadvantaged by imbalanced datasets.

Model Selection

- Choose models carefully: Different AI models have varying capabilities and limitations. Select a model that aligns with your goals and minimizes potential bias.
- Regularization and fairness techniques: Use regularization techniques and algorithms designed to promote fairness and reduce bias.

Explainable AI (XAI)

- Implement explainable AI methods: Utilize techniques and tools that provide transparency into the model's decision-making process.
- Use interpretable models: In cases where transparency is critical, consider using interpretable models that produce understandable results.

Bias Detection and Mitigation

- Regularly test for bias: Implement bias detection tools and frameworks to identify and measure bias in AI outputs.
- Bias mitigation strategies: Develop strategies to mitigate bias, such as re-sampling, re-weighting, or re-ranking data points.

Continuous Monitoring

- Implement ongoing monitoring: Continuously monitor AI systems in real-world applications to identify and address bias and fairness issues.
- User feedback: Encourage users to report concerns and provide feedback on system outputs.

Ethical Guidelines and Protocols

- Develop and follow ethical guidelines: Define and adhere to ethical AI principles that prioritize fairness, transparency, and responsible AI deployment.
- Establish review processes: Implement protocols for reviewing and auditing AI models for potential biases and

ethical concerns.

Diverse Development Teams

- Promote diversity in AI teams: Diverse teams can bring different perspectives and reduce the likelihood of bias in the development process.
- Bias training: Provide training and education on bias awareness to AI developers.

Public Disclosure

- Disclose model intentions and limitations: Clearly communicate the intended use of AI models and their limitations to users and stakeholders.
- Publish research: Share research findings, methodologies, and bias detection measures with the public.

Third-Party Audits

Consider third-party audits: Independent audits by external organizations or experts can provide an unbiased evaluation of AI systems.

Regulatory Compliance

Comply with data privacy and anti-discrimination laws: Ensure your AI system adheres to relevant data privacy regulations and anti-discrimination laws, such as GDPR and the Fair Housing Act.

Bias Impact Assessment

Conduct bias impact assessments: Assess the potential impact of AI systems on different user groups and take action to address any disparities.

Transparency and bias reduction in AI models require a multidisciplinary approach that combines data collection and preparation, model selection, ongoing monitoring, ethical guidelines, diversity in development teams, and compliance with regulations. These practices can help build AI systems that are more transparent, fair, and trustworthy.

Intellectual property rights of AI-generated works: Who owns the rights created by artificial intelligence systems?

One of the crucial legal issues surrounding generative AI is the ownership of intellectual property rights. The ability of AI systems to create new works without human input raises questions about who owns the rights to these creations and how to protect them from infringement. Some argue that AI-generated works should be considered "orphan works" and not subject to copyright protection since the creator cannot be identified. Likewise, there have been some court cases where it was held that an AI under patent law.

This scenario raises concerns about the lack of protection for such works and the potential for their misuse. To address this issue, one potential solution is to create a new category of intellectual property rights specifically for AI-generated works. But that would make an additional layer of intellectual property rights that need to be attributable to someone and might limit the exploitation of artificial intelligence.

The same applies to synthetic data, which are artificially generated by AI systems rather than collected from real-world sources. For example, who owns the rights to synthetic images if an AI system generates synthetic images based on real-world images? This raises questions about the rights of the creators of the original data, as well as the rights of the creators of the synthetic data. And the matter is already leading to disputes.

Legal liability of artificial intelligence systems: Who is responsible when AI-Generated decisions are wrong?

As AI systems become more advanced, they will exponentially make decisions that can have significant consequences, such as diagnosing medical conditions, approving loans, and even driving our vehicles. There are some regulatory restrictions, and, for instance, in the healthcare sector, an AI system is not "licensed" to provide medical treatment and, therefore, can only support practitioners. Likewise, street regulations are framed to ensure that drivers always are in control of their vehicles, even though some accidents of the last years prove that someone is abusing the potential of self-driving cars.

And privacy-related regulations provide that individuals have the right not to be subject to automated decisions and, in any case, to seek the review of such decisions by a human being, which has been amplified in Italy for AI systems used to monitor workers with the so-called Transparency Decree.

In case of mistakes due to errors in the AI system, questions arise about who is responsible for that. Some argue that the creators of the AI system should be held liable, while others suggest that the AI system itself should be held accountable.

A specific liability regime for artificial intelligence is pivotal to fostering its exploitation.

The question is whether such proposals reach the right balance between making companies accountable for mistakes caused by artificial intelligence and avoiding burdensome obligations that might hinder the growth of AI.

The development and deployment of AI systems involve processing personal data in different ways for different purposes. You must break down and separate each distinct processing operation, and identify the purpose and an appropriate lawful basis for each one, in order to comply with the principle of lawfulness.

Whenever you are processing personal data – whether to train a new AI system, or make predictions using an existing one – you must have an appropriate lawful basis to do so.

Different lawful bases may apply depending on your particular circumstances. However, some lawful bases may be more likely to be appropriate for the training and / or deployment of AI than others. In some cases, more than one lawful basis may be appropriate.

Conclusion

It is your responsibility to decide which lawful basis applies to your processing; you must always choose the lawful basis that most closely reflects the true nature of your relationship with the individual and the purpose of the processing; you should make this determination before you start your processing; you should document your decision; you cannot swap lawful bases at a later date without good reason; you must include your lawful basis in your privacy notice (along with the urposes); and if you are processing special categories of data you need both a lawful basis and an additional condition for processing.

<u>DISCOVER YOUR WRITING POTENTIAL WITH ARCCHIE</u>

We all possess unique talents for articulating various subjects, and you're among those gifted individuals. Whether you're a budding writer or a seasoned author, ARCCHIE PUBLICATIONS offers an ideal platform for your creative endeavors. If you aspire to become an author with ARCCHIE, we invite you to explore authors.arcchieonline.com and submit your application today. Our team is dedicated to assisting you in embarking on your authorship journey. Alternatively, scan QR code and connect with us.

Chapter 7

Generative AI- as a Threat to Security

As we continue exploring Generative AI and Prompt Engineering, we are constantly amazed by the innovative and creative possibilities these technologies offer. Yet, alongside their incredible potential, there lies a significant responsibility—a responsibility to recognize and address the risks they present, particularly in terms of security.

In this chapter, we shed light on a critical aspect of Generative AI that often goes unnoticed: its potential as a security threat. As we navigate this intricate landscape, we uncover various dimensions of this challenge, underlining the existing vulnerabilities and the urgent steps we must take to safeguard against them.

Generative AI, with its transformative ability to generate text, images, and code, has the potential to revolutionize industries and streamline processes. However, this very capability also opens doors to potential misuse, with one of the most alarming concerns being the creation of convincing but false information, known as deepfakes. These can be used to spread misinformation or even to impersonate individuals, leading to grave consequences for individuals and organizations.

Furthermore, the use of Generative AI in cyberattacks is a growing concern. Malicious actors can employ these technologies to generate convincing phishing emails or to bypass security measures by creating fake credentials. Such attacks can have devastating effects, compromising sensitive information and damaging trust in digital systems.

Another concern is the potential for bias in AI-generated content, which can perpetuate harmful stereotypes or discriminate against certain groups. If left unchecked, this bias can exacerbate societal inequalities and undermine the trustworthiness of AI systems.

To address these challenges, we must take a proactive approach to security. This includes implementing robust authentication measures to verify the authenticity of AI-generated content and developing techniques to detect and mitigate the impact of deepfakes. Additionally, ensuring transparency and accountability in AI development can mitigate bias and foster trust in these technologies.

The following topics will be covered in this chapter:

- Understanding the Threat Landscape
- Guarding Against Generative AI Threats

Understanding the Threat Landscape

Generative AI has shown a new phase of innovation in artificial intelligence, bringing advanced models such as ChatGPT that can produce text that resembles human language. This technology has found a multitude of applications in content creation, chatbots, and recommendations. However, while Generative AI has many benefits, it also poses potential risks that can harm security. Technology can be used for malicious purposes, which poses a significant risk to security. As a result, it is essential to assess the potential risks associated with Generative AI and identify ways to mitigate them.

Social Manipulation

One of the most significant risks associated with Generative AI is social manipulation. Malicious actors can use AI-generated content to impersonate individuals, create convincing fake news, and manipulate public opinion. The implications for elections, public discourse, and trust in digital media are profound.

Social manipulation is using deceptive or manipulative tactics to influence individuals or groups, often maliciously. Regarding Generative AI, social manipulation can take on new and concerning dimensions, posing a significant threat to security.

Generative AI technologies like text and image generators can create highly realistic and convincing content. This content can be used to deceive and manipulate individuals, leading to a range of security risks. One of the most prominent examples of social manipulation using Generative AI is the creation of deepfakes. Deepfakes are AI-generated images or videos that appear to depict real people saying or doing things they never actually did. These can be used to spread false information, defame individuals, or incite violence, which can have profound security implications.

Another way in which Generative AI can be used for social manipulation is through the creation of fake reviews, comments, or social media posts. These can be used to artificially inflate the reputation of a product, service, or individual or to discredit competitors. By manipulating public perception, malicious actors can gain an unfair advantage or undermine trust in legitimate entities, leading to financial or reputational harm.

Furthermore, Generative AI can impersonate individuals or create fake identities. This can be used for malicious purposes, such as spreading misinformation, conducting fraudulent activities, or even committing crimes in someone else's name. The ability to create realistic fake identities poses a severe security risk, as it becomes increasingly challenging to verify the authenticity of individuals online.

Social manipulation using Generative AI can also target vulnerable individuals or groups, such as those with limited digital literacy or who are easily influenced. By exploiting psychological vulnerabilities or social dynamics, malicious actors can manipulate these individuals into taking actions that are harmful to themselves or others. This can include engaging in risky behavior, disclosing sensitive information, or participating in illegal activities.

It is essential to develop robust detection and authentication mechanisms to mitigate the threat of social manipulation using Generative AI. This includes developing tools to detect deepfakes and other forms of AI-generated content and implementing strong authentication measures to verify the authenticity of online identities. Additionally, raising awareness about the risks of social manipulation and promoting digital literacy can help individuals recognize and resist these manipulative tactics.

Phishing Attack

Generative AI, a technology that can be harnessed to create highly convincing phishing emails and messages, poses a real threat. These attacks are not easy to spot, as the AI can mimic the tone, style, and content of legitimate communications. Imagine a marketing company that needs to generate product descriptions for hundreds of items in its online catalog. Instead of hiring a team of writers, it turns to Generative AI to produce unique and compelling descriptions for each product. This scenario illustrates how easily Generative AI can be misused for malicious purposes.

Phishing attacks, a form of cybercrime where attackers impersonate legitimate entities to deceive individuals into providing sensitive information, are a significant security threat. These attacks, often executed through email, messaging platforms, or fraudulent websites, can be amplified by the capabilities of Generative AI, making them even more sophisticated and challenging to detect. This heightened threat level underscores the urgent need for individuals and organizations to be proactive in their security measures.

Generative AI, with its ability to create realistic text, images, and other content, can be leveraged to enhance the effectiveness of phishing attacks in various ways. One of the most alarming methods is the creation of highly convincing phishing emails. Attackers can exploit Generative AI to generate emails that closely resemble those from legitimate sources, making it challenging for recipients to differentiate between real and fake messages. This detailed explanation of the threat highlights the need for robust security measures to counteract it.

For example, Generative AI can create emails that appear to come from a person's bank, requesting them to update their account information. The email may include official logos, formatting, and language typically used by the bank, making it difficult for the recipient to discern its fraudulent nature.

Generative AI can also create fake websites that closely resemble legitimate ones. These websites can trick users into entering their login credentials or financial information, which can be used maliciously. They can be generated quickly and at scale, allowing attackers to target many individuals simultaneously.

Furthermore, Generative AI can personalize phishing attacks, making them even more convincing. By analyzing publicly available information about a target, such as their social media profiles, attackers can create tailored phishing messages that appear more legitimate and relevant to the recipient.

Another concerning aspect is the potential for Generative AI to automate phishing. Using AI algorithms to analyze responses from previous phishing campaigns, attackers can refine their techniques and create more effective phishing messages. This automation allows attackers to scale their operations and target more individuals with minimal effort.

To protect against phishing attacks enhanced by Generative AI, organizations and individuals must remain vigilant and adopt robust security measures. These measures include educating users about the dangers of phishing, implementing email authentication protocols such as SPF, DKIM, and DMARC, and using email filtering technologies to detect and block phishing emails.

Additionally, organizations can use AI-driven tools to analyze email traffic and identify potential phishing attempts. These tools can help detect phishing emails that may have slipped past traditional security measures, allowing organizations to take proactive steps to mitigate the threat.

Deepfakes

Generative AI can create deepfake videos and audio recordings that appear genuine. This threatens privacy, reputation, and national security when used to create fake speeches or interviews.

Deepfakes are synthetic media created using Generative AI techniques that manipulate or generate visual and audio content to make it appear that someone said or did something they did not. These videos, images, or audio clips are often compelling and can be used to spread misinformation, defame individuals, or deceive people for malicious purposes. While deepfakes can be created for entertainment or artistic purposes, their potential as a threat to security is a growing concern.

One of the main risks deepfakes pose is their ability to deceive and manipulate individuals and society. For example, a deepfake video of a political figure making inflammatory statements could be circulated online, sparking unrest or influencing public opinion. Similarly, deepfake audio could be used to impersonate someone in a phone call, tricking individuals into divulging sensitive information or committing fraudulent acts.

Another security concern is the potential for deepfakes to be used in cyberattacks. For instance, a deepfake video could create a fake endorsement from a company executive, convincing employees to take actions that compromise security, such as clicking on a malicious link or sharing confidential information. Similarly, deepfake audio could be used to impersonate a colleague or supervisor, leading to unauthorized access to sensitive information or resources.

Deepfakes also have the potential to undermine trust in institutions and media. As technology advances and deepfakes become more convincing, it may become increasingly difficult to discern real from fake, leading to a general sense of skepticism and uncertainty. This erosion of trust could have far-reaching implications for society, affecting everything from elections to financial markets.

Addressing the threat of deepfakes requires a multi-faceted approach. One key aspect is the development of technologies to detect and authenticate media content. Researchers are working on methods to analyze videos and images for inconsistencies or artifacts that may indicate manipulation. Additionally, efforts are underway to develop digital watermarking and blockchain technologies that can be used to verify the authenticity of media content.

Another important aspect is raising awareness and educating the public about the existence and potential dangers of deepfakes. By teaching people how to recognize and verify media content, we can reduce the impact of deepfakes and mitigate their potential to cause harm.

Automated Cyberattacks

AI can be weaponized to automate cyberattacks, including password cracking, DDoS attacks, and malware development. The speed and precision of AI-driven attacks raise cybersecurity concerns.

Automated cyberattacks refer to malicious activities conducted by automated scripts or bots, rather than human operators, to exploit vulnerabilities in computer systems or networks. These attacks can range from simple, such as brute-force password attacks, to highly sophisticated, leveraging advanced techniques to evade detection and maximize damage. Generative AI, with its ability to create realistic and convincing content, poses a significant threat in the context of automated cyberattacks.

In this regard, one of the most concerning aspects of Generative AI is its potential to generate convincing phishing emails and other forms of social engineering attacks. Phishing attacks typically involve impersonating a trusted entity to deceive individuals into disclosing sensitive information such as passwords or financial data. With Generative AI, attackers can create highly realistic emails that mimic a legitimate sender's writing style and tone, making them more likely to trick recipients.

Moreover, Generative AI can be used to automate the creation of malware. Malware refers to malicious software designed to infiltrate or damage a computer system. By using Generative AI, attackers can generate variants of malware that are more difficult to detect by traditional antivirus programs. These AI-generated malware variants can evolve, adapting to security measures and increasing their chances of success.

Another concerning use of Generative AI in automated cyberattacks is the creation of fake news and disinformation campaigns. Attackers can manipulate public opinion, spread false information, and create social unrest by generating realistic news articles, social media posts, or videos. These campaigns can be particularly effective when targeted at specific groups or individuals, exploiting their biases and vulnerabilities.

Generative AI can also be used to automate the reconnaissance phase of an attack. Reconnaissance involves gathering information about a target, such as its network topology, software versions, and security measures. By analyzing publicly available data, attackers can identify potential vulnerabilities and devise more targeted and effective attack strategies.

Organizations and individuals must implement robust cybersecurity measures to mitigate the threat of automated cyberattacks using Generative AI.

This includes:

- Regularly updating software and systems.
- Using robust authentication methods.
- Educating users about the risks of phishing and other forms of social engineering.

Additionally, security professionals should stay informed about the latest developments in AI and cybersecurity to anticipate and counter emerging threats.

Guarding Against Generative AI Threats

Guarding against Generative AI threats is crucial as AI becomes more powerful. These threats include misuse, bias, and privacy concerns. Misuse can happen when AI is used for harmful purposes. Bias occurs when AI favors certain groups or ideas unfairly. Privacy concerns arise when AI collects or uses personal information without consent.

To protect against these threats, several measures can be taken. First, developers must design AI systems with ethical principles in mind. This includes considering the impact of their technology on society. Second, there should be transparency in how AI systems are developed and used. This helps build trust with users and stakeholders.

Another critical step is to ensure that AI systems are secure. This involves protecting them from hackers and other malicious actors. Additionally, AI should be continuously monitored and updated to address new threats.

Ethical AI Development

Ethical AI development is about creating artificial intelligence (AI) systems that are fair, transparent, and respect privacy. It involves considering the social and moral implications of AI technology and making decisions prioritizing the well-being of individuals and society.

One critical aspect of ethical AI development is ensuring fairness. This means that AI systems should not discriminate against individuals or groups based on characteristics such as race, gender, or socioeconomic status. Developers can achieve fairness by carefully selecting and preparing data used to train AI models, testing for bias, and implementing measures to mitigate any biases.

Transparency is another essential principle of ethical AI development. AI systems should be designed so that users understand how they work and why they make certain decisions. This helps build trust and allows users to hold AI systems accountable for their actions. Developers can achieve transparency by documenting the design and implementation of AI systems, providing explanations for their decisions, and making information about their systems accessible to the public.

Privacy is also a critical consideration in ethical AI development. AI systems often rely on large amounts of data, including personal information, to function effectively. Developers must implement measures to protect this data and ensure that it is used appropriately. This includes obtaining consent from individuals before collecting their data, anonymizing data when possible, and implementing robust security measures to prevent unauthorized access.

In addition to fairness, transparency, and privacy, ethical AI development also involves considering the broader societal impacts of AI technology. Developers should be mindful of how their technology will affect individuals, communities, and society. This includes considering issues such as job displacement, economic inequality, and the potential for AI to be used for malicious purposes.

Guarding against generative AI threats is a crucial aspect of ethical AI development. Generative AI refers to AI systems that can create or generate content, such as images, text, or audio, that is indistinguishable from human-created content. While generative AI has many potential benefits, such as aiding in creative tasks or generating realistic simulations, it poses significant risks.

One of the main risks of generative AI is the potential for misuse. For example, generative AI could create fake news articles, videos, or images that are difficult to distinguish from actual content. This could spread misinformation or manipulate public opinion. To guard against this threat, developers should implement measures to verify the authenticity of content generated by AI and detect and prevent the spread of fake content.

Bias is another potential threat to generative AI. AI systems learn from data, and if the data used to train a generative AI model is biased, the model may produce biased output. For example, a generative AI model trained on text from the internet may learn and reproduce stereotypes or prejudices present in the data. To guard against this threat, developers should carefully select and prepare training data to minimize bias and implement measures to detect and mitigate bias in AI-generated content.

Privacy concerns are also relevant when it comes to generative AI. For example, generative AI systems could create realistic-looking images of individuals who do not exist, raising questions about using such images without consent. To guard against this threat, developers should implement measures to protect individuals' privacy, such as obtaining consent before using their likeness in AI-generated content.

Robust Authentication and Verification

Enhanced authentication methods, such as multi-factor authentication (MFA), are crucial in minimizing the risks associated with AI-generated impersonation. In today's digital world, where interactions occur primarily online, ensuring the authenticity of users and content is more important than ever.

AI-generated impersonation refers to instances where artificial intelligence is used to mimic or impersonate real individuals or entities. It can manifest in various forms, such as fake social media profiles, fraudulent emails, or even voice and video deepfakes. These impersonations can be used maliciously, such as spreading misinformation, committing fraud, or manipulating public opinion.

One way to combat AI-generated impersonation is using MFA. MFA adds an extra layer of security by requiring users to provide two or more forms of verification before gaining access to an account or system. It can include something they know (such as a password), something they have (such as a security token), or something they are (such as a biometric identifier like a fingerprint or facial recognition).

By implementing MFA, organizations can significantly reduce the risk of unauthorized access, even if an attacker has obtained a user's password through phishing or other means. This is because the attacker would also need access to the second factor of authentication, which is much harder to obtain.

However, while MFA can help mitigate the risks of AI-generated impersonation, it is not a foolproof solution. Attackers are constantly evolving their tactics, and there have been instances where even MFA has been bypassed. Therefore, it is essential to complement MFA with other security measures, such as regular security audits, employee training, and advanced threat detection technologies.

Another crucial aspect of combating AI-generated impersonation is strengthening verification mechanisms to distinguish real from AI-generated content. This can be challenging, as AI-generated content can be incredibly realistic and difficult to differentiate from genuine content.

One approach is to develop sophisticated algorithms to analyze content for signs of AI manipulation. These algorithms can look for subtle clues, such as inconsistencies in writing style, unnatural video behavior, or anomalies in biometric data. By detecting these clues, AI-generated content can be identified, and appropriate action taken.

Additionally, educating the public about AI-generated impersonation and how to spot it can be beneficial. By raising awareness, individuals can be more vigilant and skeptical of online content, reducing the impact of AI-generated impersonation.

AI Auditing and Monitoring

Constant monitoring and auditing of AI systems is crucial to keep them safe and secure. Imagine you have an intelligent system that helps you make decisions, like suggesting what movie to watch or what book to read. If this system is not monitored regularly, it might start behaving strangely, like suggesting things you don't like at all. This could be a sign of something wrong with the system; someone is trying to manipulate it, or there's a bug causing it to malfunction.

By constantly monitoring the AI system, we can catch suspicious patterns or anomalies. An anomaly is something that is not normal, like suddenly getting movie suggestions that are completely different from what you usually like. When such anomalies are detected, they are flagged, which means they are marked for further investigation. This is like a red flag that tells us, "Hey, something might be wrong here. Let's check it out."

Detecting these anomalies early is essential because it helps us prevent any malicious activities. Malicious activities are actions done intentionally to harm someone or something. For example, if someone is trying to manipulate the AI system to show biased results, it could lead to unfair outcomes. By monitoring the system closely, we can prevent such actions and keep the AI system fair and unbiased.

Auditing is another important aspect of keeping AI systems in check. Auditing means examining the AI system's performance and behavior to ensure it works as intended. It's like checking the system's report card to see if it's doing well or if areas need improvement. By auditing the system regularly, we can identify any weaknesses or vulnerabilities that malicious actors could exploit.

Public Awareness and Education

Raising awareness about AI-generated content is essential. People need to know that this kind of content can be used in harmful ways. When people are aware of AI-generated content, they can better protect themselves from its misuse.

One of the critical ways to raise awareness is through education. By educating the public about AI-generated content, we can help people understand what it is and how it can be used. This includes teaching people how to recognize AI-generated content and report it if they encounter it.

Recognizing AI-generated content can be tricky because it can look very similar to human-generated content. However, some signs can help people identify AI-generated content. For example, AI-generated content may need more personalization or contain errors a human would not make.

Once people recognize AI-generated content, they must know how to report it. Reporting AI-generated content can help prevent its spread and protect others from being misled. Reporting mechanisms can vary depending on the platform, but most platforms have a way for users to flag content as potentially AI-generated.

Educating the public about AI-generated content and how to recognize and report it can empower individuals to protect themselves and others from its misuse. This can help create a safer online environment for everyone.

Security by Design

Incorporating security by design principles into developing artificial intelligence (AI) is crucial. When we talk about security by design, we mean thinking about security from the beginning of the AI development process. This approach ensures that security is not an afterthought but is instead integrated into every step of the development process.

By adopting security by-design principles, we can create AI systems more resilient to cyber threats. These systems are designed to anticipate and defend against potential security breaches rather than just react to them after they occur. This proactive approach helps minimize the potential harm that AI systems can cause.

One critical aspect of security by design is continuous assessment and adaptation to emerging threats. Cyber threats are constantly evolving, so our security measures must evolve, too. This means regularly updating and patching AI systems to protect against new vulnerabilities.

Generative AI, which is a type of AI that can create new content, poses unique security challenges. While Generative AI has the potential to revolutionize many industries, such as art, design, and writing, it also has the potential to be misused. For example, Generative AI could be used to create fake news articles or misleading images.

Prompt Engineering is another area where security by design is crucial. Prompt Engineering involves designing prompts or instructions that guide the output of a Generative AI model. By carefully crafting prompts, developers can control the output of the AI model and ensure that it behaves safely and ethically.

As we delve deeper into the complexities of Generative AI and Prompt Engineering, it's important to remember that these technologies come with great power and a great responsibility. We must use these technologies wisely and ethically, ensuring they are used for the greater good and not malicious purposes.

Together, we can harness the transformative potential of Generative AI and Prompt Engineering while safeguarding our digital landscapes against any threats they may pose. By incorporating security using design principles into AI development and continuously assessing and adapting to emerging threats, we can create a more secure digital future for all.

Conclusion

In this chapter, we have explored the profound impact of Generative Artificial Intelligence (AI) on security, highlighting its potential benefits and significant challenges. We began by defining Generative AI and discussing its various applications, emphasizing its ability to create highly realistic and convincing content, including text, images, and audio. While this technology can potentially revolutionize numerous industries, including entertainment, marketing, and design, it poses serious security threats that must be addressed.

One of the primary concerns surrounding Generative AI is its potential for misuse in creating fake content, often called deepfakes. These maliciously generated media can spread misinformation, manipulate public opinion, and even commit fraud. As such, the proliferation of deepfakes poses a significant threat to the integrity of information and the trustworthiness of digital content.

Furthermore, Generative AI has the potential to automate cyberattacks, enabling hackers to create sophisticated phishing scams, malware, and other malicious tools at an unprecedented scale and speed. This presents a daunting challenge for cybersecurity professionals, who must develop new strategies and technologies to defend against these evolving threats.

To address these challenges, policymakers, researchers, and industry leaders must collaborate on developing ethical guidelines and regulatory frameworks governing the use of Generative AI. These guidelines should prioritize transparency, accountability, and protecting individuals' privacy and security.

By the end of this chapter, you have made your base and understanding of Gen AI; still, there is a long way to go. There are more insights and detailed aspects which can be referred to expand your knowledge.

JOIN US ON THE

ARCCHIE PUBLICATIONS

DISCORD SERVER

Connect with fellow readers, authors, and enthusiasts to discuss all things related to our publications and the exciting world of AI, programming, and learning. Share your insights, ask questions, and engage in vibrant discussions to expand your knowledge and inspire creativity. Take advantage of this opportunity to be part of a dynamic community dedicated to exploring the frontiers of technology and innovation. Join our Discord Server today and be part of the ARCCHIE PUBLICATIONS community!

https://discord.gg/z26SenmpEt

DISCOVER YOUR WRITING POTENTIAL WITH ARCCHIE

We all possess unique talents for articulating various subjects, and you're among those gifted individuals. Whether you're a budding writer or a seasoned author, ARCCHIE PUBLICATIONS offers an ideal platform for your creative endeavors. If you aspire to become an author with ARCCHIE, we invite you to explore authors.arcchieonline.com and submit your application today. Our team is dedicated to assisting you in embarking on your authorship journey. Alternatively, scan QR code and connect with us.

9 788819 661274 0